FILL YOUR CUP FOR
CHRIST

D1715638

FILL YOUR CUP FOR
CHRIST

*A Spiritual Journey Sown &
Grown through Sports*

KRAMER SODERBERG
WITH FOREWORD BY BRAD SODERBERG

To my Mom and Dad who planted the seed of true Christian living through the example they set and the love that they gave.

Table of Contents

3rd Quarter: The Truth

4th Quarter: The Challenge

Foreword

April 8, 2019—US Bank Stadium, Minneapolis—10:30pm

Virginia 85 – Texas Tech 77

We did it! National Champions! What a game, what a season, what a team! After 33 years as a college basketball coach my dream had come true. I was a part of a National Championship team. For the rest of my life I will cherish the experience of competing in front of a crowd of over 72,000 fans on the grandest stage college basketball has to offer. As the confetti fell and "One Shining Moment" rang from the speakers—I embraced players, coaches, friends, and family members as tears rolled down my cheeks. While standing at center court posing for a picture with my wife and children, my oldest grandson in my right arm and the National Championship trophy in my left—I remember thinking to myself, "It doesn't get any better than this!"

The celebration in the locker room was electric and emotional. I'll never forget the arm in arm circle of team members, coaches, staff, and former UVA players—tears, hugs, dances, and high fives were filling the room.

The party continued back at our team hotel as I was able to gather with my brothers and sisters, my nieces and nephews, my in-laws and friends. *Pure Joy!*

April 9, 2019—St. Olaf's Catholic Church, Minneapolis—6:30am

I am a "cradle Catholic." Born into a Catholic family, attended Catholic schools, was raised by Catholic parents. For the past

20 years of my life I have tried to attend Mass on a daily basis. It has changed my life!

So, after the greatest day of my coaching career with only a couple hours of sleep I made the chilly walk to St. Olaf Church for Tuesday morning Mass. As I've learned over the years, weekday Masses are often sparsely attended—usually anywhere between 10 and 100 people. As I knelt for a few minutes of reflection and thanksgiving before the service began, I couldn't help but notice the drastic contrast between the little church and the mammoth arena I was in less than 12 hours earlier. The packed arena was full of electricity and excitement—the church had about 20 people on their knees bowed in quiet prayer. The previous night's game was seen by millions of people around the globe—the Mass would be celebrated by the small gathering of folks in a dimly lit chapel.

Promptly at 6:30am we received a warm greeting from a middle-aged priest and the Holy Sacrifice of the Mass commenced. Sleepy-eyed and cold I wrapped up in my jacket and focused my attention on the seemly ordinary service in front of me. The Mass continued just like every other one I had attended my whole life.

However, on this particular morning, as the priest held the consecrated host and the chalice of wine in his hands, raised them above the altar and recited the Eucharistic prayer, "Behold the Lamb of God, behold Him who takes away the sins of the world. Blessed are those called to the supper of the Lamb,"—I was profoundly struck by the majesty of what was taking place a few feet in front of me. Jesus Christ, the Son of the living God, was really, truly, substantially before me—body, blood, soul, and divinity! There He is, my Savior and King!

I had been mistaken the night before as I reveled in the excitement of a career defining win. There is something bigger than winning a National Championship—and by the grace of God, I am able to receive it daily as a child of God in the Holy

Catholic Church. As the priest pressed the sacred host in my hand and I drank from the chalice of Jesus' blood I stood corrected—"It doesn't get any better than *this!*"

I think it is safe to assume that most parents are very proud of their children. I know I'm certainly proud of my three kids. However, I wonder how many fathers would say they are jealous of their son. By the grace of God, Kramer and I share a genuine love of Jesus and have a profound devotion to the Catholic Church. My jealousy for Kramer stems from the fact that he cultivated this love and devotion so much earlier in his life than I did. Oh, how I wish I would have taken my spiritual life more seriously when I was his age. As this book makes very clear, he is passionate about his faith, committed to understanding the teachings of the church, and is inspired to share it all with others.

I take particular joy in seeing how Kramer has taken the lessons he's learned as an athlete and coach and applied them to his faith life. The challenging message of this book, to *Fill Your Cup for Christ*, mirrors the mindset you find in all successful athletes. The difference, however, is profound—becoming the best Christian one can be is infinitely more important than becoming the best athlete one can be!

Find the motivation, embrace the struggles, seek the truth, and don't be afraid to accept the challenge! I hope you enjoy the book.

Kramer, I love you!

—Brad Soderberg
Assistant Men's Basketball Coach
University of Virginia
2019 National Champions

Introduction

Let's make this vividly clear right from the get-go: I am not a biblical scholar, a spiritual guru, or a theologian. I am an ordinary college basketball coach who has fallen head over heels in love with Jesus Christ. I am a former athlete who discovered that the greatest and most rewarding challenge I will ever face lies not on the court, but in Christ. I am a father who has been made aware of the immeasurable gifts that a spiritual life centered on Jesus has to offer. I am a husband who by way of the world was lost, by way of grace was found. And I am a cradle Catholic who after years of spiritual sleepwalking has rekindled the fire of the Holy Spirit given to me 30 years ago on the day of my baptism.

When the thought first popped into my head to write this book, a corresponding thought quickly followed, "Stupid idea! You can't write a book, and even if you could why would you?" If I was a gifted writer, then maybe. If I was a highly knowledgeable Christian speaker, definitely. If I was a famous college basketball coach, now that makes sense. However, despite all my doubts and uncertainties I decided to start writing anyway.

As words turned into pages, pages into chapters, and chapters into sections I began to worry that I didn't have a clear idea of who I was writing this book for—but I carried on anyway. After completing the book, my concern became a reality when several professionals in the publishing world told me, "You don't know who your target audience is." After wallowing in my own rejection afflicted self-pity, I finally swallowed my pride enough to realize that all those publishing companies who turned down my book were right—I had no idea who this book was written for. Is this book just for men? Did I write this book for young adults? For athletes? Is this book for Catholics or non-Catholics? Is it for seekers of Christianity or those who already have a grasp of their faith?

I assume most experienced authors probably know the answer to this question well before they even start writing their books. However for me, a first time writer who had no clue what in the world he was doing, my approach ended up being a bit different. Eventually, through prayer and contemplation, I came to a somewhat surprising realization—I wrote this book for myself.

I wrote this book for the teenage me who thought the religion I was born in to was just a painful chore. I wrote this book for the immature college me who became lost in the ways of the world and forgot how much God loved me. I wrote this book for the professional me who was overwhelmed with all the anxiety and fear that came with the ups and downs of having a career. I wrote this book for the uninformed me who thought that Christianity was whatever I wanted it to be, or whatever I felt most comfortable with. I wrote this book for me the spouse, and me the parent who didn't realize that every moment no matter how dull or ordinary was an opportunity to glorify God—an opportunity to change the world. Finally, I wrote this book for me, the lukewarm Christian, who was content with being a mediocre Catholic unaware that God wasn't ok with me being average—but was calling me, instead, to strive for greatness.

My story isn't amazing or miraculous. I haven't received any divine visions or spiritual apparitions. This is a story of a very ordinary life in which Jesus quietly and continually called my name, and by His grace, I imperfectly responded as He slowly pulled me closer and closer to Him. Through joys and sorrows, trials and tests, successes and failures, I found myself becoming drawn to the Man I used to only think about once a week because my parents told me to.

Spiritually speaking, I have only scratched the surface of what I need to learn to fully grasp the enormity of what being a Catholic Christian means. However, in a world full of confusion, in a world overloaded with lies and quite literally empty of the truth—perhaps a normal, very average, father of three, husband, and coach is exactly what our Church needs right now. Someone who can present spiritual strategies, biblical insight, and Church teachings in "laymen's terms." Someone to shed some light on the truth and beauty of our faith. Someone to present the idea that you don't have to be a priest, a nun, or an 80-year-old grandma (who you think has nothing better to do than go to Mass every day) to discover and live out the teachings of Jesus Christ and reap the wonderful spiritual gifts that His Church has to offer each and every one of us.

Jesus tells us, "You shall love the Lord your God with all your heart, with all your soul, with all your mind, and with all your strength" (Mark 12:30). By these words, it seems as if Jesus is proposing that there are different ways to love God, different forms in which our love for God can manifest itself. My hope is that this book will challenge and inspire all those who read it to love the Lord more completely. I hope you will learn to love the Lord with all your HEART, through your emotions, feelings, and desires. To love the Lord with all your SOUL, showing your love for Christ through your spiritual practices and your commitment to prayer. To love the Lord with all your MIND, by growing in an intellectual understanding of Christ and His Church. And finally, to love the Lord with all your STRENGTH, pouring out your love of

Christ through the works and deeds that you perform for His sake and His glory.

Those acquisition editors and publishing companies were right, I have no idea who my target audience is. But, I think that is just the way God wants it. If this book, by God's grace, helps just one young teenager realize that they are not alone and that Jesus loves them beyond their wildest dreams, glory to God! If this book brings home just one fallen-away Catholic or rekindles the spiritual fire of just one sleepwalking cradle Catholic, glory to God! If this book reassures and comforts just one suffering soul in the midst of trial or pain, glory to God! If this book sparks the desire of just one non-Catholic Christian to more deeply investigate their faith, ask questions, and find answers, glory to God! If this book inspires just one person to turn away from the ways of the world and pursue a life of true Christian holiness, then, I say, Glory to God in the Highest!

God Bless you on your journey to find the fullness of our Christian faith—which is the everlasting, indescribable, uncontrollable, inexhaustible love of our Lord and Savior, Jesus Christ.

Prologue

I was in 6th grade, my father a college basketball coach, had a year and a half prior gotten relieved of his duties as interim head coach at the University of Wisconsin and moved us to St. Charles, Missouri. Now the head coach at St. Louis University, he was running a summer basketball camp for grade school kids that I was gladly participating in. Being a coach's son my entire life, I became enamored with that which I was constantly around, the game of basketball. So a summer basketball camp was exactly where I wanted to be. On this particular day, my Dad decided to bring all the campers together to talk with them. I wondered, as I am sure most of the 5th through 8th graders at the camp did, why we had to sit down and listen to a speech instead of playing knock out or five on five. And especially for me, the last thing I wanted to do was listen to my Dad talk for twenty minutes.

Once the 150 to 200 kids were finally settled and seated at center court of the rec center my Dad blurted out in his loud, attention-grabbing voice that only coaches possess: "Today, I'm going to introduce you to some basketball players!" This statement quickly grabbed the attention of all the antsy grade-schoolers, myself especially. I was excited because I assumed he was going to introduce a few of his college players who I had come to know and admire from my time around the team. Also egotistically excited in my desire to gain the approval and awe of my fellow campers, I would be very proud to tell them that I know the players and they know me.

But to my dismay, my Dad had no intention of bringing out any of his players. To our confusion he began to dig around in his backpack, apparently looking for something or someone. From the hidden confines of this secret pack he yanked out a cup. A cup? "Campers, say hello to Big John!" Among muffled giggles and confused smiles, we all responded in a somewhat confused manner, "Hello, Big John." Picture in your mind the 64oz. guzzlers that you can get from most gas stations for 99 cents, that's what my Dad was holding up in his hand. He continued, "This is Big John he is a basketball player and he is six foot eight inches tall, he's really strong, very athletic, he can jump up above the rim and dunk it any time he wants." He proceeded to set Big John on the table that was set up in front of him. Back to the backpack he went, this time pulling out another cup. But this one was a little smaller, more like the size of a normal drinking glass. He said, "Now this is Jimmy. Jimmy isn't quite as tall as John, he's about 6'3, he is a pretty good athlete, and he is very strong. He has very long legs and long arms, perfect for playing defense." Again, just like with Big John, my Dad set Jimmy on the table in front of him.

For a third time my Dad reached in his backpack and pulled out another cup, this one looked like a Dixie cup. Holding the tiny cup between his thumb and his index figure he said, "This is little Tony. Now, unlike Big John and Jimmy, Tony isn't very tall—he's only 5'9". Tony isn't very athletic, he can't jump high like John or run very fast like Jimmy. Tony isn't all that strong either, he is still pretty thin and not very muscular." Setting little Tony on the table next to the other two cups, all of us campers got a good look at the discrepancy of size between the three cups and most especially the difference of size between little Tony and the other two. Bewildered by why my Dad introduced us to three basketball players that turned out to be cups, I sat there a little disappointed and very confused.

After a long pause, giving us all time to look at the cups and ponder where this could be going he continued, "Now, Big John, although he is big, strong, and athletic, he is also pretty lazy. John doesn't work very hard at practice and sometimes doesn't even show up. When Big John does come to practice, he only tries his best when he knows his coach is watching. He doesn't practice much on his own. Big John only does the very minimum." Then to our surprise one of the assistant coaches brought over a pitcher full of water and my Dad poured about two ounces of water into the giant 64oz. cup. My Dad went on, "Now Jimmy, he isn't as lazy as John. He tries very hard at practice and shows up every day. But Jimmy doesn't do much extra, he doesn't practice on off days and only works out when he feels like it." Again, grabbing the pitcher of water my Dad poured about six ounces of water into the cup, filling it up about half way. He continued, "Now little Tony is different. He shows up to practice every day, usually thirty minutes early and always stays late. During practice he plays as hard as he can every drill. He works out on his own all the time, practicing his shot and working on his ball handling. He lifts weights five days a week and runs sprints up and down his street to get in better shape. Little Tony is the hardest worker you will ever meet."

Then my Dad began to pour, the image still ingrained in my mind. The water quickly filled to the brim of the tiny Dixie cup. He continued to pour and water started to over flow past the edge of the cup. Soon water spread on the table and started dripping onto the floor. He set down the pitcher, looked at the mess he made and then looked at all of us, "I want you all to understand one thing—it doesn't matter how much potential you have, how high you can jump, or how fast you can run. It doesn't matter if you are tall or short, strong or weak. It doesn't matter if everyone thinks you'll be successful or no one does.

It does not matter how big your cup is! All that matters is how much water you put in your cup."

I can still feel my heart beating, feeling as if he was talking directly to me. Energy and adrenaline hit me like a fret train. In that moment my mind and my heart told me that I could accomplish everything I wanted as long as, "I filled my cup to the top!" I played the rest of camp that day with the image of those cups playing over and over in my mind. I played as hard as I could, trying to fill my cup, just like Dad told me to.

On the thirty minute drive home from St. Louis to St. Charles that afternoon, I told my Dad about all the good plays I made and the contests that I competed in. As we were getting close to home I could feel my Dad beginning to get serious, I fell silent and waited for him to speak—knowing he had something important to say. "Kramer, you know that story I told today?" Nodding in approval, "Yea Dad, it was really good!" The car went quiet for another moment and then my Dad said something I wasn't expecting, "Kramer, you are little Tony..." As a 6th grade kid who still thought he was going to grow to be 6'5, I realized for the first time that I was pretty short (and due to my gene pool, probably wouldn't grow much more). I was not very strong, or fast, and didn't have the God given gifts that would allow me to be a 6'8" basketball Phenom.

"But Kramer that does not matter! All that matters is that you get the most out of the potential that God has given you. All that matters is that you fill your cup to the top." He knew my aspirations to play Division 1 college basketball, to start as a freshman on the high school varsity team, to be player of the year in the state, to win a state championship, and to make it to the NBA. But, he also understood how hard it would be for me to accomplish all those things. "Kramer, your success will not be measured by how many of your goals you achieve or the recognition you get or don't get. Success lies in one thing and one thing only, filling your cup to the top. If you do everything you possibly can to become the best player you can be, if you push yourself every day to improve, if you never give up in your pursuit of that—you will be a success. If after your basketball career is over and you haven't achieved any of the goals on your list, but you filled your cup—you are a success! Fill your cup to the top, son, make sure at the end of your career your cup overflowing." Now let's begin our spiritual journey together. *And don't worry, we'll get back to the cups...*

1st Quarter: The Motivation

Chapter 1: All you need is Love

Any journey, challenge, or adventure that anyone has ever embarked on always begins with one thing—love! Nothing in all of human history has ever motivated or driven mankind like love. More than money or fame. More than greed, vengeance, or lust. Love is the single greatest motivator for anyone who is pursuing anything.

The man who ends up being an astronaut started as a young boy who fell in love with outer space—with stars, planets, rockets, and aliens. He became hooked on the mysteries of the universe, and that love allowed him to never stop pursuing what he loved. That famous vocal artist who amazes audiences with her incredible voice was first a little girl who loved to sing. Who loved to get dressed up, stand on the couch, and perform for her audience of two—mom and dad. That superstar football player who is on the cover of magazines and billboards was first a young boy who fell in love with a game and loved it so much that he just couldn't stop playing.

Why does anyone decide to take a trip to Hawaii? Because they love the beach and the warm weather and the smell of the ocean. Why does anyone decide to help shelter stray dogs? Because they have fallen in love with animals, and out of that love they pursue any opportunity to help them. Why would anyone get married (perhaps the most challenging journey anyone can take)? Because they have fallen in love, and because of that love they want to share their entire self with only one person for the rest of their life. Nothing anyone has ever pursued has started and then been accomplished for any reason other than love. Now, many people may have thought they were in love but never were. Or someone may have been in love with something at some point and fallen out of love after a while. But no one has ever started a journey, pursued a challenge, persevered through struggles, and accomplished a goal for any other reason than love. As Saint Paul says to the Corinthians, without love "I am nothing" and without love "I gain nothing" (1 Corinthians 13:2-3).

This is where the spiritual life begins and ends. Love is why so many people have given their lives for the sake of Christianity. Love is why so many people fight for the Church and the beliefs instilled in them from the Church. Love is the catalyst, the starting point, the end all be all of the spiritual life. Now the opposite can also be said: A lack of love is why so many people have given up on Christianity. A lack of love is why so many people have left the Church or why some people feel like living a spiritual life is no longer necessary. A lack of love is why so many good-intentioned Christians who attempt to focus more on their faith lives quit before they bear fruit. So many of us want to grow more in our spiritual lives and desire to re-commit our life to Christ. Most of us want to go on a journey to find Jesus, or desire to achieve spiritual peace. But so many of us give up on those wants and desires solely because of our lack of love. We lose the desire to pray when prayer becomes monotonous, to trust when life gets difficult, to come to Mass when we just don't feel like it, and to strive for holiness when holiness becomes inconvenient, unpopular, or unappreciated.

The issue that most people have in their pursuit of growing stronger in their Christian faith is that they have never fallen in love. They have yet to fall deeply in love with the one thing our faith is all about, *Jesus!*

I don't care how much you desire to find peace, how committed you are to daily prayer, how much you know what a difference going to Mass can make in your life. I don't care how many Lenten promises or New Year's resolutions you have made, or how badly you don't want to go to Hell. If you aren't head over heels, out of your mind, crazy in love with Jesus Christ—you will always resort back to your previous way of life. You will always give up on your pursuit of the true Christian life.

As a new year begins I am writing these words, and at this very moment many good people are looking to better themselves through a stronger more deliberate spiritual life. I'm sure many are committing to a New Year's resolution of praying each morning for thirty minutes or to start to go to Church again. I have to believe that countless people are saying this is the year they are going to commit to being a better Christian. I know this because I have done it in the past, and I know from experience that most of these people will achieve their resolution for the first several weeks or maybe even for a month. But sooner or later the desire that they had on January 1st will begin to fade away, because the desire is not driven by love.

I struggled in my spiritual life for quite some time. I desired to find peace and fulfillment through my faith. But every time I made an attempt to grow as a Christian or to commit to my Catholic faith, my desire would never last. Whether because my parents, priests, or teachers were emphasizing the wrong things or because I just wasn't listening (probably the 2nd one)—I had come to the understanding that being Catholic meant: going to Church, following commandments, confessing my sins, saying my prayers, knowing all the religious terms, memorizing the Our Father, receiving the Eucharist, and passing all my religion tests. Now don't get me wrong these are all great things, important things we should strive to do. But those are the things that nurture your faith, things that you desire to do only after realizing what Christianity is really about. I failed many times trying to strengthen my faith life because I thought by just following the commandments, saying my prayers, and going to Church I would find meaning in my Christian faith. These things gave me no joy, no excitement, no desire, or determination. Being Catholic was just a chore, no matter how hard I tried to make it something more.

If you truly desire to take steps in your spiritual life, if you truly want to grow as a Christian and make your faith the center of your life you need to do one thing first—fall head over heels in love with Jesus Christ!

The turning point of my uninspired spiritual life was through the help of a wonderful servant of God, a holy priest named Father Hampe, the chaplain at the hospital in my home town. I initially started going to Sunday Mass at the hospital chapel because I had heard that Father Hampe's homilies were only like 5 minutes long—and as a flaky Catholic, a shorter Mass was always a better Mass. After going once or twice I found out the rumors were true. But I quickly realized the crowd at this Mass wasn't big because the homily was short. People filled this tiny chapel out the door because Father Hampe was a master homilist, always speaking about the one thing people desired most, Jesus. No matter what the readings were, no matter what day of the liturgical year it was, when you heard a Father Hampe homily you heard about Jesus. You heard about how much He loved you, how much He desired an intimate relationship with you, and how by just falling in love with Jesus your life could change for the better.

This was the first time in my life I began to recognize Jesus not as a historical character or a cosmic ghost-God. But as a real, living, loving person who was waiting ever so patiently and at the same time ever so anxiously for me to realize that I could have an amazingly profound and indescribably intimate relationship with Him. That's what it means to be a Christian!

Falling in love with Jesus is the beginning, middle, and end of the Christian life. If you want to grow in your spiritual life, if you want to find meaning and excitement in the Catholic Church there is only one place to start, and that's with Jesus. Fall in love with Jesus and everything else will come with it. As Pope Saint John Paul II once said, "In comparison to the love of Jesus, everything else is secondary. And without the love of Jesus, everything else is useless."[1] Once you fall in love with Jesus, once you desire Jesus over anything else, going to Church, following commandments, and loving your neighbor will become things that you do—not because you think you should, or because your parents or your priest said you have to—but because they are great ways to be closer to Jesus, great ways to tell Jesus you love Him. Once you have fallen in love with Jesus you yearn to please Him, you desire to be with Him, and you will do anything to draw yourself as close as possible to the person that you love most.

To try to make this point come to life, I want to tell another story that my Dad so wonderfully relayed to me:

It was 1992, and most coaches trying to advance in the business and grow in their profession make their way to the coaches' convention at the Final Four each year. This particular year my Dad happened to sit in on a presentation where the speaker was discussing motivation, drive, desire, and the pursuit of goals. As most young coaches would do, he made his way up to the front of the auditorium eager to learn and take notes. After the keynote speaker had started his speech, discussing all the worldly desires that being a successful college coach had to offer—money, fame, prestige, etc. To my Dad's surprise the man pointed at him and asked him to come to the stage. Taken aback, and a little unsure, my Dad reluctantly walked on to the stage.

After getting asked his name, where he was from, and where he coached, the keynote speaker asked my Dad a more personal question. "Do you have any kids?" My Dad responded proudly, "Yes! My son Kramer just turned 3 years old." With a smile and a congratulations the speaker continued. "Ok, Brad, I want you to imagine there is a balance beam on the stage, just like the one you have seen the gymnasts use in the Olympics." Nodding his head, my Dad gestured that he understood and was imagining the beam there on stage. "Now Brad, if I put 50 bucks on the middle of that beam, would you walk across the beam if you got to keep the money in the middle?" My Dad responded quickly, "Sure, no problem! I'll take 50 bucks." The speaker nodded with a smile, and continued. "Now Brad, imagine I put that same balance beam across two basketball rims (10ft high) and there is 5,000 dollars in the middle—would you walk across for that?" A little less sure of himself, my Dad responded slowly, "Uh, yea I think I would be able to shimmy across there for 5,000 dollars without falling off and breaking my leg." With an impressed looked for my Dad's bravery and a nod, he continued, "Ok Brad, what if that same balance beam stretched across the roofs of the world trade center buildings and I put a million dollars in the middle, would you walk it?" My Dad half laughing and half bewildered quickly responded, "No way! Are you kidding me?" Then the speaker upped the ante, "What about 100 million?" Still laughing my Dad responded, "No chance!" Retorting again the speaker said, "What about a billion dollars Brad, 1 Billion Dollars!" A little confused by the redundancy of the questions my Dad responded, "I wouldn't walk across that beam for all the money in the world. I'm not going to risk dying! Are you kidding me?"

As the other coaches in the audience still giggled and whispered thoughts to one another, the speaker became quiet as he slowly walked away from my Dad who was standing in the center of the auditorium stage. After a long moment to gather his thoughts, the speaker turned to my Dad and in a quiet, almost concerned voice said, "Brad, Kramer is out there and the only way to save him is to walk across, would you go?" The auditorium fell silent and as tears welled up in my Father's eyes, he said, "In a second, no question about it!"

Finally my Dad and all the other coaches in attendance understood what this dialogue was all about. They finally understood the point the speaker was trying to make: if what you are chasing in this life isn't driven by love something will always stop you from pursuing it. Whether you are pursuing a career for money or fame, a big house or fancy cars. If you are pursuing a friendship or a marriage for comfort, security, or intimacy. If you are pursuing a spiritual life for peace and respect, or out of obedience and moral fiber. If you are pursing anything for any other reason than love, you will at some point find yourself in a place where you will no longer want to pursue your goal.

Every great pursuit whether professional, personal, or spiritual will face trials, challenges, and difficulties. Any goal that you chase will have days of frustration, monotony, and confusion. Every journey that we could ever attempt to undertake will present us with times in which we desire to let up, to walk away, to quit. Saint Augustine once said, "While all sorts of setbacks are encountered as difficult by those who do not love; those who do love, on the contrary, find them trivial and easily manageable. There is no suffering, however cruel or violent it may be, which is not made bearable or even reduced to nothing by love."[2] Stated similarly, "When we rise to respond to God's love, the obstacles disappear; on the other hand, without love even the tiniest difficulty seem insuperable. If there is union with the Lord, everything becomes tolerable."[3]

The only thing that will hold you firm in your pursuit of anything is love. Money, fame, and honor cannot motivate the way love does. Security, comfort, or peace cannot motivate the way love does. Pleasure, intimacy, lust cannot motivate the way love does. Anger, vengeance, pride, self-interest, ego—none of these can motivate the way love does. If you want to grow as a Christian, if you desire to go on the difficult journey to achieve a true and profound spiritual life, start with this one thing first: *Fall in love with Jesus!*

Chapter 2: You are SO Loved

What so many of us fail to realize when we embark on a spiritual journey is that this is not a quest to convince God to love you, or to make Him realize that you deserve to be loved. Saint Catherine of Siena once said, "God does not love us in spite of our weaknesses, He loves us because of our weaknesses."[4] God isn't standing on a thrown in heaven with His arms crossed looking down on you, waiting for you to kiss His feet. God isn't someone you have to chase or track down. *God is the pursuer!* Our God desires us, and He chases us. He is not demanding us to pursue him. He is constantly and continually pursuing us out of His great love and devotion to His most beloved creations. It was once said, "God is to man as the ocean is to a grain of sand. The only difference is the ocean doesn't love the grain of sand."[5] The question is, do you realize how much you are loved?

Two images that we see constantly throughout the Bible is the image of a father loving his child and a groom loving his bride. What Jesus is desperately trying to pound into our heads is that we are loved in the same way that a good father loves his child, in the same way that a groom loves his bride.

If you have ever been to a wedding you have surely witnessed the moment when the doors of the Church open and the bride is presented to the assembly and most importantly to the groom, for the first time. Most people tend to look at the bride at this time. Have you ever watched the groom the moment he sees his bride for the first time? Imagine the look on the groom's face as the back doors of the Church open and he sees his bride. What you'll see is sheer joy glowing on his face. You'll see unconditional love, and anticipatory excitement in his smile. You'll see tears welling up in the groom's eyes as he readily awaits the opportunity to give his life completely to the person he loves most.

Now I want you to imagine that same look that is on the groom's face, on the face of Jesus. Imagine all those emotions that were running through the groom's mind running through the mind of Jesus. Imagine those same tears that welled up in the groom's eyes, falling from the eyes of Jesus as He watches *you* walk towards Him, fully ready to commit your life to Him. We are the bride and Christ is the groom, and He is looking at you with excited, tear filled eyes, because He loves you with a love that you cannot comprehend. "For as a young man marries a virgin, your Builder shall marry you; And as a bridegroom rejoices in his bride so shall your God rejoice in you" (Isaiah 62:5).

The great Catholic apologist Scott Hahn describes this wedding imagery in his book, *The Lamb's Super*, "We are the bride of Christ unveiled; we are His Church. And Jesus wants each and every one of us to enter into the most intimate relationship imaginable with Him...He uses wedding imagery to demonstrate how much He loves us, how close He wants us to stay and how permanent He intends our union to be."[6] We as individuals and we as the Church are the bride of Christ Jesus. Jesus looks directly at you with the loving eyes of a groom who is anxiously awaiting his bride at the end of the aisle. Saint Teresa of Avila once said, "Christ does not force our will. He takes only what we give Him. But He does not give Himself entirely until He sees that we yield ourselves entirely to Him."[7] Jesus is ready to give His entire self completely over to you. But, you must first make that walk down the aisle toward Him. You must be willing, as He is, to offer your entire self, your entire life over to Him.

Next, how often in scripture do we hear Jesus talk about God in terms of a Father? Countless times in the Gospels and all throughout the Bible we see images and parables about a loving Father. "As a father has compassion on his children, so the Lord has compassion on those who fear Him" (Psalm 103:13). When asked by his disciples, "Lord, teach us to pray..." Jesus respond by saying, "When you pray, say: *Father...*" (Luke 11:1-2). Soon thereafter Jesus compares God to a father giving to his son, "What father among you would hand his son a snake when he asks for a fish?...If you then, who are wicked, know how to give good gifts to your children, how much more will the Father in heaven give the Holy Spirit to those who ask Him?" (Luke 11:11-13).

Jesus wants us to realize that God is our Father and that God loves us as a good father loves his children. This is the sole purpose of the famous parable of the prodigal son. Although this parable is called the prodigal son, "it's really a story about the father"[8] more than it is about the son. A father who anxiously awaits the return of his disobedient son: "While he was still a long way off, his father caught sight of him, and was filled with compassion. He ran to his son, embraced and kissed him" (Luke 15:20). "In describing the father in this way, Jesus is telling us about His Father, what His Father is really like. It is a shocking revelation of the superabundance of the Father's love, a love that is so far beyond our comprehension, that what Jesus is telling us makes the Father almost look ridiculous. 'But if you really want to know what God is like. He is like the father I have just told you about. You will never be able to understand the immensity of His love. So do not be afraid of Him.'"[9] God is an anxious Father waiting for *you*, His beloved son or daughter, to come home. And when He sees you, in His joy and ecstasy, He runs to you and embraces you in His Fatherly love.

If God is our Father, then we are his children. Jesus' apostles continually speak of this idea throughout the New Testament as a message of great joy and great hope: "See what love the Father has bestowed on us that *we may be called*

11

children of God. Yet so we are" (1 John 3:1). "And I will be a Father to you, and you shall be sons and daughters to Me, says the Lord Almighty" (2 Corinthians 6:18). "But to those who did accept Him He gave power to become children of God, to those who believe in His name" (John 1:12). We are all children of God. And as Jesus instructed us to do, we must "become like little children" (Matthew 18:3) in the way we look at our Heavenly Father. We must look at God the way a little child looks at their father or their mother—with love, trust, joy, dependence, and awe. All parents know that unique look of love and trust that only their young children can give to them. After seeing that same look from my own son, I realized that the way he looked at me was the same way I was called to look at God. Because of my son's example, I felt compelled to write this poem:

If in search of true life as My sons and My daughters
Just look to a child, who so loves his father.
His eyes follow his father wherever he goes
His father's love is forever; this, yes, he knows.

When he is frightened his father will comfort his fears
And when he is crying, dry all of his tears.
He depends on his father for food and for clothes
His father's love is forever; this, yes, he knows.

He knows that at night his father will put him to bed
And when the sun rises awake him again.
When he's tossed in the air, he knows he's just fine
For his father will catch him each and every time.

When he scrapes up his knee, one kiss is the cure
His father's love is forever, he knows this for sure.
When he sees his father's face, pure joy you will see
His father's love is forever, always to be.

A child's love never stops and trust never fades
That's why they're first in My kingdom and best ever made.
So if you're searching to make it to Heaven above
Just look to a child full of trust, joy and love.

Chapter 3: How do you look at God?

Do you look at God the way the child in my poem looked at his father? When you think about God, what image comes to mind? Do you see an image of an unimaginable being far off in the distance who has no interest in you? Do you see an image of an angry God who will impose His wrath on you if you don't do what He wants? Do you see an image of a God who is only pleased with you when you live a perfect life? Or are you seeing an image of a God who doesn't care about you, isn't proud of you, and isn't looking out for you? If you were to imagine God speaking to you right now, would you hear a condescending and disappointed voice or a proud and loving voice?

When Jesus was baptized and came up out of the waters of the Jordan River the heavens were opened and a voice came from heaven saying, "This is my beloved Son, with whom I am well pleased" (Matthew 3:17). These words that God spoke of Jesus are the same words that God speaks of you. God says directly to you, 'You are my beloved son/my beloved daughter, with whom I am well pleased.' He doesn't just say this after you have lived a perfect life, or done a good deed, or committed your life fully to Him. God says these exact words about every person on earth, no matter what stage in their life they are in. Whether you are in perfect communion with the Church or not, whether you are struggling with sin or not, whether you feel loved or not—God calls you His beloved child.

You exist for no other reason than because God loves you. God didn't create you because He needed to fill a void in His life—God has everything He needs within His own self. God doesn't need any of us. But because of how much God loves you, He chose to create you. Hear the words of God speaking directly to you: 'You are My beloved son,' 'You are My beloved daughter, with whom I am well pleased.'

God is a proud Father, the proudest of fathers. He raves about you. He wants everyone to know all the beautiful and unique qualities that He has given you. He wants to tell the world all the wonderful things you have done, are doing, or will do. Can you hear God in heaven right now?

> *"Hey, Abraham! Anthony just forgave a person he had held a grudge against for many years! I knew he would."*

> *"Elijah, take look at Bethany. What a great job she is doing raising her children!"*

> *"Gabriel, come and see! Steve just gave his life to Jesus! All those times he turned away from Me, I always knew he would come back. What a wonderful son he is!"*

God is like one of those overbearing parents who can't help but beam about their child. He is like that parent who constantly talks about all that their kid has done or achieved— going on and on about their amazing personality traits and talents. God is like that parent who delights over all the simple qualities and basic achievements that are so small and minuscule that most of us would think they aren't even worth mentioning. As a college basketball coach I constantly have parents tell me about how great a basketball player their son is. These parents will tell me how well their son can dribble and shoot and that if I were able to see him play, I would be very impressed. Most of the time after watching their son play, in my head I think, "I'm sorry Ma'am/Sir, but your kid really isn't that good." God is that parent! He raves about the things that we may find insignificant, unimpressive, or unimportant.

Picture God in heaven grabbing Moses as he just so happened to walk by and while holding him around the shoulder points down and says:

14

"Take a look at Samantha. She just received an A on her first big math test! She is so smart!"

Or telling Saint Mother Teresa or Saint John Paul II:

"Did you hear about Maurice? He was just given a promotion at work! I'm so proud of him. He worked so hard for that."

Or interrupting a group conversation between a host of angels:

"Sorry to interrupt guys, but I had to tell you, Kim and Angie just made amends after all these years! I knew they would. They are such wonderful women!"

You can almost see everyone in heaven rolling their eyes at God, saying, "Yea, yea we know your kids are great, we know how much you love them." But it doesn't stop there. God isn't just invested and proud of His children who are succeeding or who are doing good deeds. God cares about, is invested in, and is proud of those people who are struggling, those people who have made some poor decisions, and those people who are dealing with difficulties. God sees the best in all of us, and desires for all of us to become the best we can be. God knows our hearts, and knows our struggles. He is a compassionate and proud Father who loves us no matter what. Does your image of God allow you to see Him saying things like this?

"Jesus, Greg just stole from the liquor store again. But don't worry, I know he has a big heart full of love. He's going through some difficult challenges right now, but I know he will find his way. He's a good kid deep down. I just love him so much!"

God pulls Mary aside:

"Mary, did you hear, Jackie had to check into a rehab center. It's ok though, I know who she

really is. She is going to turn it around, she is
such a wonderful person. She is so strong. Pray
for my daughter, Mary."

God looking down with a tear in His eye after hearing one
of his children say that he doesn't believe that God exists:

> *"O Frank, you may not believe in me right now,*
> *but I believe in you. I know the confusions and*
> *trials that you have gone through that have*
> *brought you to this point. But I will never leave*
> *you, I will never give up on you. I love you my*
> *son, come home!"*

I'm sure for most of us, this is not how we often think of
God. It is against our cultural training to think like this. We
are trained to think that what we accomplish: how much
money we make, or how much attention and honor we receive
determines our worth. When you begin to truly understand
how much you are loved you begin to realize who God truly is.
If you, as a father or a mother, know how much you love your
children or you children know how much your mom and dad
loves you—take that love and multiply it by 100 billion and
after doing that you may have found a tiny sliver of how God
feels about you. In the words of Fr. John Ricardo, "Life is
supposed to be lived in a response to the love that I've already
come to know, opposed to, living in such a way as to get God
to love me."[10] Understand, my brothers and sisters, how much
you are loved by God. Once you do that, you will be ready to
love God in return.

Chapter 4: Love at First Sight?

Falling in love. How does it happen? Where does it start? I'm not sure if the old saying, "Love at first sight," is true or not. But, I have to believe that if you talked to every person in the world who has ever fallen in love, a majority of them would not say they were completely, 100% in love the moment they saw someone. I would say a more accurate statement would be, "intrigued at first sight" or "enamored at first sight." For me personally, the first time I met my wife was in 6th grade on the playground of St. Cletus School. She was playing soccer and asked me, the new kid, if I wanted to play with her and her friends. I'm sure I was thinking that she was cute, and that I liked that she played sports—but I know I wasn't in love with her the very moment I saw her. Or similarly, how a young woman who happens to notice a handsome man at a coffee shop reading one of her favorite books is probably intrigued by that man, I doubt she is fully in love. At least for most people, love doesn't happen in an instant. Love is a process. People fall in love after learning more about a person, spending time with that person, seeing their personality, finding out about their interests, and by coming to know who they really are deep down.

After reading the last three chapters I hope that many of you have a deep desire to fall in love (or more in love) with Jesus. But a desire to fall in love doesn't mean that you instantly are in love. There isn't a magic command or a secret prayer that will make you suddenly fall in love with God. Love doesn't work that way. Loving Jesus takes the same work, effort, and time that it does to love anyone else in your life.

When a young child becomes obsessed with something, whether it be sports, dinosaurs, or princesses—when a child finds something that really intrigues them, what do they do? They start asking questions about it. They ask mom and dad to buy them toys and clothes related to it. They want to watch movies that are only about that one thing that has intrigued them so much. If you're asking yourself, how do I fall in love with Jesus? Start by falling back on the advice we heard two chapters ago, "become like a little child." Start in the same place that the little boy who became obsessed with dinosaurs does, or do the same things that the little girl who was fascinated with princesses would do.

If you want to fall in love with Jesus, ask questions about him and find the answers. Read the Gospels and listen to Jesus' words. Find all the books and movies you can that talk about Him—and most importantly, spend time with Him. Nothing can help us fall in love with someone more than spending time with that person. If you want to fall in love with Jesus, spend time with him, talk to him, ask him to reveal himself to you, go to Church. Don't wait, start now! Your pursuit of Jesus won't be a waste. If you truly and wholeheartedly seek to know all you can about the one we call the Son of God, sooner or later you will find yourself more in love than you have ever been in your life.

When my oldest son was just about 2-years-old, I showed him the movie Space Jam (Michael Jordan joins Bugs Bunny and the Looney Tunes to defeat the evil aliens who stole the talents of the NBA players)—and if you haven't already seen this movie and didn't already know all that I just said, please stop reading this book now and go immerse yourself in a classic! Now back to the story, I showed my almost 2-year-old son Space Jam and he enjoyed it more than me (if that was even possible). He wanted to watch it again and again. The more he watched it the more he realized how awesome Michael Jordan was, and he started to want to know more about him. So I started showing him Michael Jordan highlights on the computer, and he grew more obsessed. We gave him Michael books, Jordan clothes, shoes, and posters and he just could not get enough. All my son wanted was to be like Michael Jordan.

Then, on his 2nd birthday I decided to rock this little boy's world with the greatest gift he had ever received. I bought him a red Michael Jordan jersey with the game shorts included, and he lost his little mind. From that moment on my son, at least in his mind, had become his hero. He would shoot hoops in our living room yelling, "I'm Michael!" If we called him by his actual name he would correct us with, "No, I'm Michael!" If we ever wanted him to do anything that he didn't want to do we would tell him that the real Michael Jordan does it: "Michael Jordan always ate all his food at dinner," "Michael always listened to his mom and dad," "Michael never hit his friends." Nothing motivated my son more than his desire to be just like the person he had come to love so much. He wore his red Michael Jordan jersey every day for the next ten months. Well, actually we had to buy him a white and a black Michael jersey also, because the red one needed to be washed. But he wore a red, white, or black Michael Jordan jersey every day for the next ten months. Every day!

Become like a little child towards Jesus. Become obsessed with Jesus like my son became obsessed with Michael Jordan. Read the books, watch the movies, and ask the questions. Take the time to learn about Jesus, if you do that you will undoubtedly fall in love with Him—and after you fall in love, this amazing thing will happen, just like it did with my son, you will start to want to be just like Jesus. You will want to act just like He acted. You will want to talk just like He talked. And you will want to treat others just like He treated others.

Let's all become like my son saying, "I'm Jesus!" When someone calls us by our name let's all starting thinking, "No!

I'm not Jake, I'm Jesus!" "I'm not Katie, I'm Jesus!" Let's all start being like little children.

Nothing says that we can't wake up every morning and put on our Jesus jersey and walk around each day pretending to be Jesus. And guess what? This Jesus jersey doesn't need to be washed, we can't grow out of it, and it is a one size fits all kind of jersey. Put that jersey on each day when you wake up and make a statement to the world, "I'm Jesus!"

Chapter 5: Let's Talk about Jesus

What is the foundation of our faith? What brought about this Christian movement? What has given rise to hospitals, charities, and universities? Why have so many given their lives to serve the poor, feed the hungry, and clothe the naked? What started all this? Where did all this come from? How did the greatest movement in human history come to be? How did the most powerful organization in the history of mankind begin? You can answer all those questions with one name, Jesus! So let's talk about Jesus!

What do you really know about Jesus? Do you fully know all that you possibly can about the man we call our Savior? Do we as Catholics have an understanding of who He was as a person? Do we as Christians know how He lived, spoke, acted, and prayed?

As humans we all have an instinctual desire to define people, to put them into categories, to describe them to others. We are constantly interpreting people's looks, actions, and words in order to put them in a box and characterize them. He or she is very quick-tempered, funny, prideful, or dramatic. He or she is a worry wart, a class clown, a Debbie downer. Although judging others is not something that we as Christians are called to do. There is no question that through the actions and words of others we can come to a pretty solid understanding of who that person is and what that person is about—good or bad.

So if we do this so often and so easily with others in our life, why can't we do the same with Jesus? If we are so often describing ourselves to others, whether in a job interview or after first meeting someone at a party—why can't we use the same human characteristics to describe Jesus that we use to describe ourselves and others? Jesus was in fact fully human, which means He did have human qualities and characteristics.

Have you ever taken the time to characterize Jesus as you would a new co-worker or new class mate? Have you ever gone through the Gospels and looked at Jesus' words and actions in great depth, and then taken all the circumstantial evidence that you have found and written a list of human characteristics that He possesses? Have you ever tried to describe Jesus to another person, maybe to someone who doesn't know Jesus, or to a child who asks, "What is Jesus like?"

This experiment/activity is something that all Christians should take the time to do. Whether you are first starting your faith journey and have never opened the Bible or whether you are a long time Christian who feels like you know all you need to know about Jesus. Take the time to read through the Gospels and every time Jesus speaks listen closely and take a characteristic of him from His words. Every time the Gospel writer describes something that Jesus did, put yourself in that scene and draw a conclusion about who Jesus is from His actions. By taking the time to really learn about who Jesus is and what character traits He possesses you will not only become fascinated by this man, but you will begin to fall in love.

If each of us were to sit down and write out all of our own characteristics, we would have a long list of traits that could accurately describe who we are. We would all have characteristics that we are proud of—things that are good, decent, and holy traits. However, if we were being honest, we would all have characteristics that we would not be so quick to reveal. If we all sat down and thought about who we truly are, each of us could list traits that are unholy, negative, and some just downright despicable. Our negative traits might be anger, laziness, egotism, or lust. We might be a person who is constantly anxious, jealous, or depressed. Perhaps we lack the traits of kindness, humility, or patience. You might be a person whose negative qualities far outweigh your positive ones, or you may be a person who has just one or two bad character traits that you can't seem to rid yourself of. No matter who you are or what your list of traits may be, we are all flawed humans. We all have a list of not so wonderful traits that make us ugly and sinful. But, in midst of our weaknesses, we all have wonderful God given traits that make us beautiful and holy.

Now Jesus, just like us, has a long list of character traits. But unlike us, His list is not comprised of any of the negative, unholy traits that fill up our lists. As we have been taught, Jesus Christ has truly been made one of us, like us in all things except sin. This means that as a human, He must have had human characteristics—but in the same sense, as sinless, none of those traits would have been bad, for none of those traits would have led Him to sin. Right now, take a few minutes before you go on and try to write down some character traits that you think accurately describe the Jesus that you think you know. Use all the Bible stories you've heard throughout your life, information from the things you've learned from religious classes, books, or movies and write down a list of traits that you think Jesus possesses. Write down all the words that you would use to describe Jesus to someone who had never heard of Him before.

If you took the time to do this you undoubtedly came up with a long list of traits. Honestly the list is endless. Any positive trait that we have in our vocabulary could surely be stamped on Jesus. Jesus was loving, humble, compassionate, kind, gentle, and selfless. Jesus was forgiving, faithful, trusting, and loyal. Jesus was joyful, content, and always at peace. Jesus was passionate, driven, focused, and consistent. Jesus possessed any and every trait that any human would or should desire to have. Jesus was and is all that we ought to be, all that we should strive to become. But let us look a little more deeply into scripture to find evidence of some of the characteristics of Jesus that we all came up with:

> Loving: In John 15:13 we hear Jesus say, "No one has greater love than this, to lay down one's life for one's friends." Jesus not only spoke in love, but acted in love and we see the fulfillment of His love for us when He acts on the very words He spoke. Throughout His life Jesus proved He possessed the characteristic of "loving." But at no other time did He prove it more than when He died on the cross for our sake. ***God, allow me to become loving like Christ.***

> Compassionate: In Matthew 9:36 we hear how Jesus traveled from town to town curing every disease and illness. The Gospel writer says, "At the sight of the crowds, His heart was moved with pity for them because they were troubled and abandoned, like sheep without a shepherd." His heart ached for those who suffered, He was compassionate towards those who were struggling. ***God, make me compassionate towards others as Christ is compassionate towards me.***

> Inspiring: In John 8:1-11 we see Jesus challenge and inspire a woman caught in adultery. Most of us only see the compassion of this scene, but after Jesus shows the woman great mercy we see Him present her with an inspiring challenge. Jesus in His compassion stands up for the woman being publicly persecuted by the scribes and Pharisees for the sins she had committed. And after all her accusers had walked away, no longer condemning her, we hear Jesus say to the

woman in an undoubtedly inspiring tone, "Neither do I condemn you. Go, and from now on do not sin anymore." What could be more inspiring than to have the man who just stood up for you when no one else would present you with this life changing challenge, desiring for you to be the best you can be. *God, may I inspire others, by my actions and words, to become the best they can be, just as Jesus did.*

Selfless/Serving: In Mark 10:45 we hear Jesus say, "For the Son of Man did not come to be served but to serve." And in John 13:5 we see Jesus wash the feet of His disciples. In both cases we are hearing and witnessing Jesus display the same characteristic. He is teaching His disciples and us that it is better to serve than to be served. *God, help me to be selfless in the way I serve those around me.*

Passionate: In Mark 11:15-19 we see Jesus in righteous anger driving out those who were buying and selling in the temple. We see Jesus overturn the tables of the money changers and drive out those dishonoring His Father's house. In the story of the *Cleansing of the Temple,* Jesus shows His passion for His Father and for the proper worship that He knows God deserves. *God, allow me to be passionate in my defense of what is good, true, and holy.*

Kind/Gentle: In Luke 18:16 we hear Jesus say, "Let the children come to me and do not prevent them." Jesus, throughout the Gospels, continually shows kindness to the weakest and most vulnerable of persons. *God, may I be kind and gentle in all my works and in all my interactions.*

Joyful/Funny: In John 1:46-47 we see Philip find Nathanael and tell him that they had found the Messiah and that He was from Nazareth. We hear Nathanael in a real snarky, smart aleck kind of way comment, "Can anything good come from Nazareth?" Soon-there-after as Jesus saw Nathanael coming toward Him we hear Jesus respond in a seemingly light hearted, teasing sort of manner, "Here is a true Israelite. There is no duplicity in him." I imagine Jesus with a small smirk on His face as He pokes fun at the future disciple. Throughout the gospel if you can't imagine Jesus as joyful, lighthearted, funny, and fun to be around, I believe you are missing one of the most wonderful qualities that Jesus possessed. ***God, help me to find the same enjoyment and lightheartedness in my life that Jesus found in His.***

Humble: In Luke 2:1-14 we see the birth of Jesus. Born in a stable and "laid in a manger, because there was no room for them in the inn." I'm not sure we all fully comprehend the level of humility that this simple act displayed. Remember, this is the God of the universe who by His own will came into this world not as a powerful king but as a helpless baby. This is the creator of all things who was born not in a luxurious hotel but in a stable. This is the one eternal and everlasting Being who decided to be laid not in a golden crib covered in precious jewels but in a farm animal's feeding trough. Although Jesus was the one person who deserved all praise and glory He never once asked for it, never once desired it. ***God, make me humble that I may become little in my heart, mind, and desires.***

At Peace: In Luke 4:1-13 we see Jesus led by the Spirit into the desert where He was without food for forty days. While excruciatingly hungry Jesus was tormented and tempted by the devil. During this time we never see Jesus become phased or irate. Jesus is perfectly at peace. No matter the circumstances in Jesus' life we see Him constantly and continually at ease. I can only imagine this must have been a major reason why the disciples were first attracted to Jesus. Imagine a person who walked through life with the aura of perfect contentment and peace no matter what. ***God, help me to always be at peace within myself no matter the circumstances that surround me.***

Faithful/Trusting: In Luke 22:42 we hear Jesus painfully utter the most trusting words that have ever been spoken in all of human history, "Father, if You are willing, take this cup away from Me; still, not My will but Yours be done." While brought to the point of sweating blood as He prayed knowing His coming fate, Jesus followed the plan of His Father although as we see, He so desired to not undergo all that was coming. ***God, allow me, as I undergo my own tests, to be trusting and faithful to You no matter what.***

Now, after our little character trait scavenger hunt, I hope we have come to a small understanding of some of the characteristics that Jesus lived out so perfectly during his thirty some odd years on this earth. The beauty of what we have found out about Jesus and His traits is that all of us can find traits that Jesus possessed, that we too hold as our own. The beauty of the human race is that if we look hard enough, we can find a Jesus trait in all of our brothers and sisters no matter who they are, what they've done, or how they act. At our best we all have a few of the same traits that Jesus has. At our best we all reflect the image of Jesus in certain, and sometime hidden ways.

Perhaps you know someone who is just so fun to be around, funny, lighthearted, and joyful—you're getting a glimpse of Jesus' joyful personality. Maybe you know someone who is wonderfully compassionate and helpful, always there to lend a helping hand, speak a kind word, or offer an open ear—you're seeing up close the heart of Jesus. Maybe you know someone who is driven and focused, someone who no matter what obstacles they are presented with, continue to carry on and persevere—you're experiencing the passionate fire that burned inside Jesus during His public ministry for the sake of His mission. Maybe you know a mother or a father who are so loving, so patient, and so forgiving of their children no matter what they do—you're witnessing the love and compassion Jesus has for us all. Maybe you know someone who is suffering from cancer or another serious illness, someone who even in the midst of their struggle is able to smile, laugh, and remain hopeful and faithful—you're truly in the midst of Christ, the one who suffered so perfectly for our sake.

As you walk through this world so ready to characterize others, so quick to describe the traits of those around you. Don't forget to take the time to see Jesus in the wonderful traits of those you come in contact with. Don't forget that at our best, each one of us shines the light of Jesus in our own way. There may be just one small beautiful trait hidden amongst a flurry of bad traits, but it is there, and so is your chance to get a glimpse of Jesus.

With this understanding of Jesus' traits and maybe a newfound understanding of our own traits the question now becomes, is it possible to be like Jesus? Can I take all that I know of Him from what I have read and what I have heard and apply it to my own list of character traits? Can I transform myself into a perfect reflection of Jesus? Through my actions and my words, is it possible for people when they see me, to see Jesus? Can I become just like Him?

Chapter 6: Just Like Jesus

As I mentioned earlier, my own faith life first began to show signs of life only after I started to become increasingly obsessed with Jesus. Through Father Hampe's homilies, a few life-changing books, and my own personal investigation I became enthralled—I literally could not get enough of Jesus. I wanted to hear every story, read every book, and understand every teaching. The more I learned about Jesus, the more obsessed I became. The more obsessed I became, the more I wanted to be just like Him.

As a child the first thing I remember wanting to be was a Ninja Turtle, after that phase I recall the desire to be a hockey player like the kids from the Mighty Ducks movies. As I grew older I wanted to be like all the players my Dad coached—and as I became an adult I strived to be like my Father, a man I had admired my whole life. But none of those people I looked up to in my youth had ever intrigued me like Jesus did.

As we found out in the last chapter, Jesus was and is the most amazing, fantastic, indescribable, undefinable person that, I'm sure, any of us have ever heard of. The way Jesus lived and acted fascinated me. The way He treated others and loved even those who hated and persecuted Him astounded me. The constant peace and never ending joy that surrounded Him was something that I so desired. The passion, determination, and relentless spirit that He displayed while pursuing His mission was so inspiring to me. So without even realizing it, Jesus had slowly become my hero, my idol, my role model. He became the person I wanted to be like.

Just as a child tries to mimic their favorite super hero by dressing like them, talking like them, doing all the awesome moves they do. Or the same way my son tried to act just like

Michael Jordan by learning all his moves, doing all his dunks, and even sticking out his tongue just like him. So too, I became like a little child in my awe and fascination of this man called Jesus. I wanted to imitate Christ just as Saint Paul encouraged the Ephesians to, "Therefore be imitators of God, as beloved children" (Ephesians 5:1). I wanted to learn every character trait that Jesus possessed, every different circumstantial action that He made, every word that He spoke, and how He spoke it—because in my mind, the only way to become like my hero was to mimic Him in every way I could.

So the question I then began to wrestle with was, how? How could I be like Jesus, the Son of God? Is that even possible? Or am I just being naïve and childish like a little boy who thinks he can become Spider Man. In my effort to accomplish this, I first asked the question: why was Jesus able to act so different than me, than all of us? Everything He did, every way He acted was completely opposite of what our fallen human nature tells us to do. Trying to imitate Jesus just made me realize how unholy I really was, how fallen and sinful every human being is. Perfecting just one of the wonderful Jesus traits that we talked about in the last chapter is extremely difficult. How can we possibly perfect all of them?

During this time I came across a book called, *Just Like Jesus*, by Max Lucado. The title, easily drew me in considering I had become a person completely obsessed with the notion of becoming just like Jesus. On the first page of the first chapter the author posed a question to his readers that really got me thinking. He asked, if Jesus took over your body for one day, how would you be different? If Jesus had the same life as you, the same circumstances, the same problems—would you be any different? Dumb question, of course I'd be different! But, here is the wonderful image that Lucado presented to me in his book:

"What if, for one day and one night, Jesus lives your life with His heart? Your heart gets a day off, and your life is led by the heart of Christ. His priorities govern your actions. His passions drive your decisions. His love directs your behavior.

What would you be like? Would people notice a change? Your family—would they see something new? Your coworkers—would they sense a difference? What about the less fortunate? Would you treat them the same? And your friends? Would they detect more joy? How about your enemies? Would they receive more mercy from Christ's heart than from yours?

And you? How would you feel? What alterations would this [heart] transplant have on your stress level? Your mood swings? Your temper? Would you sleep better? Would you see sunsets differently? Death differently? Taxes differently? Any chance you'd need fewer aspirin or sedatives? How about your reaction to traffic delays? (Ouch, that touched a nerve). Would you still dread what you are dreading? Better yet, would you still do what you are doing?

Would you still do what you had planned to do for the next twenty-four hours? Pause and think about your schedule. Obligations. Engagements. Outings. Appointments. With Jesus taking over your heart, would anything change?"[11]

The answer to the question is quite obvious. But these four simple paragraphs intrigued me and led me to begin to wonder, how was Jesus able to act so differently than every human being that had ever walked the earth? How did He possess all those amazing qualities? How was it possible for Him after all He had gone through, all the challenges and difficulties, for Him to act the way He did. While coming in contact with all those mean spirited people how could He possibly still have loved them? How, while dealing with erratic, loud mouthed, cowardly disciples could He have put up with them in such an understanding way? How could He have stayed faithful and trusting in God's plan although everything seemed to be going terribly wrong?

I initially answered this difficult question by saying, "Well, Jesus is the divine Son of God, so God was always with Him." I came to the quick conclusion that the reason why Jesus was able to act the way He acted was that He had His Father constantly by His side. I assumed the way Jesus was, came from the fact that God was always with Him.

At first I thought this seemed to be an acceptable answer. It explained to me in a very logical way how it was possible for Jesus to possess so perfectly all the character traits that He did. However, this answer also left me very disappointed and a little discouraged. If Jesus was only this way because he was the divine Son of God, then I had no chance of becoming like Jesus. I am definitely not divine, and if I need to be divine to be like Jesus, then I have no shot. I contemplated my initial answer to the question for a bit longer and began to find some holes in my logic. If I had concluded that Jesus was the way He was only because He was the Son of God and because of that God was always with Him—my answer just didn't add up. Doesn't Jesus tell us that God is always with us wherever we go? I knew from my time spent in a Catholic grade school and from going to Mass every Sunday during my childhood that God wasn't just this distant divine being who lived in another cosmos and paid no attention to us. I knew I had been told many times before that God was with me no matter where I went. I found the confirmation I was looking for in scripture soon thereafter:

> 1 Corinthians 3:16 tells us, "Do you not know that you are the temple of God, and the Spirit of God dwells in you?"

> In John 14:23 we hear Jesus tell us, "and My Father will love him, and We will come to him and make Our dwelling with him."

> In Romans 8:38-39 we find, "For I am convinced that neither death, nor life, nor angels, nor principalities, nor present things, nor future things, nor powers, nor height, nor depth, nor any other creature will be able to separate us from the love of God in Christ Jesus our Lord."

> And to put the icing on the cake I come to find out that the name Immanuel literally means "God with us."

Just like God was always with Jesus, so too is God always with us. So the initial way I answered the question was wrong. If it were correct wouldn't I act just like Jesus considering—as I had come to find in scripture—that both Jesus and I have God with us all the time, no matter where we go or what we do?

Why then, was Jesus so different? If just like me, Jesus was fully human, and just like me, had God with him always—why was He able to act the way He did all the time? After pondering over this question for quite some time, a light bulb finally went off in my head. Jesus is the same as us, being that He is fully human and that God is always Him. But what made Jesus different—what allowed Him to be holy and sinless—was that unlike me and unlike all of us *Jesus was constantly and continually aware of God's presence in His life.* I found out many years later that this understanding of Jesus is also taught by the Catholic Church and found in the Catechism, "In fact, all his life is a prayer because he is in *a constant communion* of love with the Father."[12]

There wasn't one second of Jesus' life where He wasn't in communion with His Father and aware of His presence. There wasn't one moment during His ministry where Jesus didn't know that His Father was with Him, leading and guiding Him

33

wherever He went. Not once during Jesus' struggles, trials, and persecutions did He forget that His Father loved Him. Every time Jesus saw someone in need, He saw His Father in them, also in need. Every moment of Jesus life He saw His Father in the beauty of creation, in the "birds of the air" or the "flowers of the field." In moments of trial and difficulty He was able to be at peace because He knew his Father was present. Even in His darkest hour, while sweating blood, He was able to say, "Not my will, but yours be done," because He knew that His Father loved Him and that His Father's plan was perfect.

After coming to this surprising and somewhat life changing conclusion, I continued to read through Lucado's book excited to learn more. When I arrived at chapter five and read the title, *"Being Led by an Unseen Hand—A God Intoxicated Heart,"* I immediately felt drawn in. And in the second paragraph of chapter five of *Just Like Jesus*, my thoughts and uneducated conclusions about Jesus and the possibility of a perfect spiritual life were manifested through Lucado's words:

> *"We are always in the presence of God. We never leave church. There is never a nonsacred moment! His presence never diminishes. Our awareness of His presence may falter, but the reality of His presence never changes.*
>
> *This leads me to a great question. If God is perpetually present, is it possible to enjoy unceasing communion with Him?...What if our daily communion never ceased? Would it be possible to live—minute by minute—in the presence of God? Is such intimacy possible?"[13]*

The remainder of the chapter introduced me to a book that would completely change the way I looked at my spiritual life: *Practicing His Presence*, which was composed of the journals of Frank Laubach & Brother Laurence. In this book both authors described their experiences as they strive to become constantly and continually aware of God's presence all the while attempting to have a "continuous inner conversation with God." In one of his journal entries, Frank Laubach, asked himself the very question I had so recently asked myself:

> *"Can we have that contact with God all the time? All the time awake, fall asleep in His arms, and awaken in His presence? Can we attain that? Can we do His will all the time? Can we think His thoughts all the time?...Can I bring the Lord back in my mind-flow every few seconds so that God shall always be in my mind?"[14]*

My thoughts concerning the reasons that Jesus was the way He was were confirmed by Lucado's brilliant words a few pages later:

> *"The same was true with Jesus. Because He could hear what others couldn't, He acted differently than they did. Remember when everyone was troubled about the man born blind? Jesus wasn't. Somehow He knew that the blindness would reveal God's power (John 9:3). Remember when everyone was distraught about Lazarus's illness? Jesus wasn't. Rather than hurry to His friend's bedside, He said, 'This sickness will not end in death. It is for the glory of God, to bring glory to the Son of God' (John 11:4). It was as if Jesus could hear what no one else could. How could a relationship be more intimate? Jesus had unbroken communion with His Father."[15]*

Thanks to the help of three brilliant theological minds—Max Lucado, Frank Laubach, and Brother Laurence—I received the answer to the spiritual question that I so desperately wanted. I was given the hope that yes, it is possible to be like Jesus. Will it be easy? No! Can I do this on my own? No! But, by God's grace and my own focused effort to be constantly aware of God's presence in my life, I can become like Jesus.

When we hear the words "pray without ceasing" in 1 Thessalonians 5:17, the idea of constant communication with God is exactly what St. Paul was presenting to the Christian community of Thessalonica. I want to challenge you today by asking: Can you live this way? Can you train yourself to be aware of God at all times, every second of every day? Can you learn to "pray without ceasing," and can you learn to live in constant discussion with Jesus? Saint John Chrysostom once said, "It is possible to offer frequent and fervent prayer even at the market place or strolling alone. It is possible also in your place of business, while buying or selling, or even while cooking."[16] Frank Laubach explained, that all this new way of living comes down to is "a matter of acquiring a new habit of thought."[17]

I have become convinced that this practice of constant awareness of God is the key to never ending contentment, peace, and joy. It doesn't mean everything in your life will always go right. It doesn't mean that pain and suffering won't ever confront you. What it does mean is that no matter what you face in this life, you will be content—even joyful—knowing that this is a part of God's plan for you and that He is with you in every moment. If you are able to become constantly aware of God—every second of every day, just like Jesus—you will find more peace, joy, contentment, thankfulness, and love than you could have ever imagined.

In his book, *A Portrait of Jesus*, Joseph F. Girzone described Jesus' human nature as the same as ours, but also explained that Jesus' constant awareness of God was what made Him something more:

> *"In His human nature He felt the same emotions we feel. He could share our pain, our worry, our feelings of discouragement and failure, but He*

*never lost trust in His Father's love and strength
which He knew He could always count on. In
that we could learn much from Him, knowing
that no matter how dismal things may look,
God's presence is not far from us. With God
nearby, what is there to fear?"*[18]

Jesus wasn't the way He was just because He was divine. Jesus was the way He was because He was in constant communication with His Father. He was constantly aware that God loved Him, and He continually sensed His Father's presence in the people and things around Him. Jesus was the way He was not because God was always with Him, but, because He was always aware that God was with Him. As Laubach so eloquently said, "He walked along the road day after day 'God-intoxicated' and radiant with the endless communion of His soul with God."[19]

Think for a second about your day. What if every person you came in contact with each day, stranger or friend, you recognized Jesus in them? What if every bird you saw, flower you walked by, or sunray that hit your skin, you realized was a gift from God? What if, every difficult moment or time of suffering you encountered in your day, you were aware that God was with you—to comfort and strengthen you? What if during every unsure and stressful moment you understood that God has your best interest in mind and that His plan for you is perfect.

Once you become constantly aware of Jesus, everything you do is done for God and with God. Listen to St. Paul's words: "So whether you eat or drink, or whatever you do, do everything for the glory of God" (1 Corinthians 10:31). Once you are in constant communion with Jesus you begin to continually feel the way Saint Mother Teresa did, "I am a little pencil in the hand of a writing God who is sending a love letter to the world."[20] And you begin to realize that everything you do is important, as St. Josemaria Escriva did when he said, "Do everything for love. That way there are no little things. Everything is big."[21]

My newfound spiritual mentor, Frank Laubach, explained that this practice doesn't come easy. But if you are able to train yourself in this spiritual awareness, you will find ultimate peace. He captured the spiritual ecstasy he received from this practice in these beautiful words:

> "This concentration upon God is strenuous, but everything else has ceased to be so. I think more clearly, I forget less frequently. Things which I did with a strain before, I now do easily and with no effort whatsoever. I worry about nothing, and lose no sleep. I walk on air a good part of the time. Even the mirror reveals a new light in my eyes and face. I no longer feel in a hurry about anything. Everything goes right. Each minute I meet calmly as though it were not important. Nothing can go wrong excepting one thing. That is that God may slip from my mind if I do not keep on my guard. If He is there, the universe is with me. My task is simple and clear."[22]

If you want to be at peace, if you want constant joy and contentment, if you want your faith life to explode—you must first fall in love with Jesus. After you fall in love with Jesus, you will without a doubt, want to be just like Him. Once you desire to be just like Him, you will strive to imitate how He lived, acted, and spoke. The first step of being like Jesus—and the only way you'll be able to imitate the Son of God—is by being aware of God every second of every day in all people, things, and situations. From the mouth of Saint Gregory of Nazianzus, "We must remember God more often than we draw a breath."[23]

Let us all strive to be just like Jesus—constantly aware that God is with us, that God loves us, and that God's plan for us is perfect.

Chapter 7: What's the Game Plan, Coach?

Many have said this before, but in the world of athletics it is especially prevalent, "A goal without a plan is a wish." I think this quote is also extremely important in regards to any spiritual journey that you decide to undertake. If after reading the first six chapters of this book you have the motivation to give your life more fully to Christ, to strengthen your relationship with Jesus, to fall more deeply in love with God, or to become more like Jesus—Glory to God! But, even if you truly want to do all these things, if you don't have a plan on how you're going to achieve them—they probably will never happen. A game plan is needed. And although I'm nowhere near the best spiritual coach you could find, I think my game plan can at least help you get started.

First, what is our game plan for falling in love (or more in love) with Jesus? Simple. Learn everything you can about Him. Remember, just like the little child who becomes enamored by dinosaurs or my son towards Michael Jordan—we must seek to find all the information we can about our subject. Falling in love with Jesus is the starting point. Read the gospels, highlight every word that He spoke. Find books that talk about Him, movies that portray Him, anything that you can get your hands on that will give you a better understanding of who Jesus was and is. All this will benefit you in your quest to fall in love with Jesus. The more information you take in about Jesus the more you will love him. There isn't one person who has taken the time to openly learn about who Jesus is that hasn't fallen in love with Him. He is irresistible!

Second, what is our game plan for strengthening our relationship with Jesus? As you continue to gather more and more information about Jesus, the more you will love Him.

However, just falling in love with Jesus intellectually isn't enough. To have a truly loving and intimate relationship with someone, you can't just love them with your mind—but must also love them spiritually and emotionally, with your entire heart and soul. How do I achieve a close friendship and intimate relationship with God? "Precisely as any friendship is achieved. By doing things together. The depth and intensity of the friendship depend upon the variety and extent of the things we do and enjoy together."[24] The only way to fall in love with Jesus spiritually and emotionally is to spend time with Him. Only through personal interaction with Jesus can your relationship with Him reach the intimacy level that He desires. *You must spend time with Christ.* Talk to Him about everything, take the time to listen to Him, ask Him for the grace to love Him more fully. Whether it is for thirty minutes when you wake up, an hour of adoration time, or fifteen minutes before you go to bed. You must create time within your day where just you and Jesus, with no distractions, get to spend quality time together.

Thirdly and finally. What is our game plan for becoming more like Jesus? The answer, as we found in chapter six, is constant awareness of God's presence in your life. But, like we learned in the last chapter that is much easier said than done. Training yourself to become fully aware of God's presence in your life is a process. This process will take years and years to perfect, and this constant awareness may be something you are never able to completely master. However, whether you are one day able to become continually aware of God's presence or not—by reaching for perfection you will surely find yourself changing for the better.

Here is the way I got started trying to become more aware of God's presence and how I first stated attempting to be in constant communication with Him. I committed to doing just three things in three very specific situations that would trigger my awareness of God throughout the day:

> Nature: Anything in nature I saw, I would allow that trigger to make me think of God. From a morning sunrise, to a bird, a flower, or a nice warm breeze. I tried to notice every simple wonder in nature—and when I did, I would take a moment to marvel at it and say, "Thank you Jesus, for this beautiful reminder of you."

> People: Any person I saw, talked with, or just so happened to walk by would trigger my thought of God and I would try to recognize Jesus within each person. Whether it was a friend or stranger, family member or vague acquaintance. No matter who it was, no matter what they looked like, or what they were doing—I would try to recognize Jesus in them. Whenever I saw or interacted with another person I would say in my head, "In this person is Jesus."

> Trials: Any moment of struggle, annoyance, or frustration would trigger my awareness of God in my life. If a moment of worry or stress reared its ugly head within my daily routine, I would think of God and quietly say, "Jesus, I offer this moment of stress to you, take care of everything."

By just having these three simple triggers throughout my day I was able to enhance my awareness of God in an instant. Now, of course, I would have lapses in my triggers or forget at times that I was supposed to think of God at certain moments. But by having those three triggers I began to recognize God and speak with Him immeasurably more than I ever had before. Without interrupting my day or my work, by adding these three simple triggers, I instantly became a more pleasant person. Automatically I became more thankful, more compassionate, more content, and more at peace. In the words of Frank Laubach, "I began to live as if there were nothing, absolutely nothing but Him."[25] I floated through my day as if Jesus was walking with me hand in hand, telling me what to say and how to act. Anything that I faced whether good or bad, simple or stressful, was easy to deal with and a joy to do.

If you want to get a little taste of how Jesus felt—the peace, joy, and contentment that he lived with every second of every day—just add those three simple triggers to your day and you will instantly become more aware of God's presence and more constant in your conversation with him.

That's the game plan, people. Those are some strategies you can use to fall more in love with Jesus, to enhance your relationship with Him, and to become more aware of His presence in your life. Now let's be clear, the game plan that works for me may not work perfectly for you. Come up with a strategy that fits your life and your needs. Find a book about Jesus that intrigues you, find a time to be alone with Jesus that fits your schedule, and come up with some triggers during the day that will make you recognize God's presence in your life.

Now that you have the game plan, it is time to execute it. Win or lose, perfect or flawed, if you have a plan to pursue Jesus and do the best you can to execute it—you will not be disappointed. "And I tell you, ask and you will receive; seek and you will find; knock and the door will be opened to you" (Luke 11:9).

Pope Francis once said, "God loves us. We must not be afraid to love Him."[26] Don't be afraid to love God, don't be afraid to love Jesus. Reach out to Him, He is calling your name. Talk to Him, confide in Him, and tell Him all of your worries and fears. Thank Him for all the good things in your life and ask Him to help you with your struggles. Jesus is in the heart of each one of us just waiting for you to begin that personal loving relationship with Him. I promise you, when you finally find yourself head over heels in love with Jesus Christ and constantly aware of His presence in your life—you will find more joy, peace, and fulfillment than you could have ever dreamed of. In the words of Saint Louis IX, "Fix your whole heart on God, and love Him with all your strength, for without this no one can be saved."[27]

Pursue our Lord because he is pursuing you. Seek our God because has never stopped seeking you. Start walking down that aisle because Jesus, your bridegroom, is eagerly waiting at the end for you. Embark on the journey because Jesus is your guide—but don't forget, on this journey you will need great motivation to climb the mountains and scale the valleys that you will undoubtedly face. But as long as you are in love you will surely succeed. For without love no other motivation will matter, however, with love no other motivation is necessary.

2nd Quarter: The Trial

Chapter 8: Take up your Cross

After becoming enthralled with Jesus and finally fully committing to my Christian faith, I assumed that life would be all sunshine and rainbows from that point on. When I first began to strengthen my relationship with Christ, I had a very prideful and unrealistic mantra: "Now that I have Jesus, now that my faith is strong, nothing can go wrong, nothing will shake me. I can handle anything, and all will be well."

Like a young athlete thinking he or she will go to college and start as a freshman, be the leading scorer, and win a championship—unaware of the hardships and struggles they are about to encounter while pursuing a new and challenging goal. Like a college valedictorian who after landing a great job thinks that in no time they will make their way to the top of the corporate ladder and be running the show without ever coming across any roadblocks along the way. Like a young married couple, who are so in love and so excited to start their lives together, think everything will be perfect—not realizing that marriage is probably the most challenging journey they will ever embark on. I was the enthusiastic, unexperienced, overzealous youth who lacked true spiritual wisdom. I thought that just because Christ was now the focal point of my life, everything I had planned for myself and my family was going to come together perfectly.

Most people who take off in their faith and commit their life to Christ find that there is always a honeymoon period. A time of great peace, joy, and contentment. A time where you are so profoundly filled with enthusiasm and gusto for your new way of life that you think nothing will ever take you off that spiritual high. However, most people at some point come to realize that just because Jesus is now a part of their life in a more profound and intimate way doesn't mean that they won't face hardships, struggles, pains, and difficulties. The great Catholic novelist, Mary Flannery O'Connor, sums up the misconception that most enthusiastic, newly formed Christians have: "What people don't realize is how much religion costs. They think faith is a big electric blanket, when of course it is the cross."[1] This quote perfectly described the understanding that I had of what my newly reformed Christian life would be. I thought that the warm fuzzy feelings of this 'big electric blanket' would last for the rest of my life and that I would be shielded from all the evils and pains that this world had to offer. Oh, how wrong I was.

I shouldn't have been blindsided by the fact that Christianity didn't just mean peace and joy—that Christianity actually and literally meant the cross! We have all heard this Bible verse before (and if you haven't make sure you take a look), but I think most of us pass over these words as if they are just a catchy Christian jingle, "If anyone wishes to come after Me, he must deny himself, and *take up his cross* daily and follow Me" (Luke 9:23).

Jesus isn't trying to trick us. He isn't a sly telemarketer who is attempting to mislead you into buying something you aren't aware you are getting. Jesus tells us, straight up, with no mixed words, that to be his disciples we must 'take up our cross.' Jesus makes it very clear that if you are going to follow him prepare yourself for hardships, for struggles, for pain— prepare yourself for the cross! In the words of Saint John of the Cross, "If anyone wants one day to possess Christ, never let him seek Him without the Cross."[2] When Jesus tells us to follow Him, He is telling us to prepare for the hardships that He faced. Jesus is saying, if you want to be my disciple you can't just follow me when things are going well, you have to follow me to the cross. Jesus tells His disciples and reminds us all: "In the world you will have trouble..." (John 16:33).

In a most perfect image of what we should expect once we truly dive wholeheartedly into our Christian faith, Jesus prepares us through the example of His own life. In the Gospels we see the gloriousness of Jesus' baptism—we see the sky opening up and the Holy Spirit as a dove descending upon Him. We hear God himself say, "You are My beloved Son; with You I am well pleased" (Mark 1:11). What an amazingly powerful moment that began Jesus' public ministry. He must have felt so profoundly motivated and enthusiastic about the mission He was now ready to undertake. And if a fictional author was going to write the next line of the story, it would probably have something to do with Jesus immediately setting out on His journey proclaiming the good news, joyfully and peacefully doing his Father's will, and finding great success in doing so. However, we all know that this isn't a fictional story and that is not what happened next. We hear in three out of the four Gospels that immediately following Jesus' baptism He was lead into the dessert to be tempted by the devil. Jesus wasn't led to a festival, or a banquet, or a fancy feast after He was baptized. After His profound spiritual encounter, Jesus wasn't presented with a path of comfort and peace. After Jesus was given His mission through the waters of baptism, He was immediately faced with a challenge, a trial, a test that we mere humans can't even fathom—forty days in the desert, with no food to eat, being constantly tormented by the devil. What a pleasant way to begin His new Christian mission...NOT!

As my players would say, "Don't get it twisted." The Christian life is more than peace, joy, and contentment. Christianity is the cross! No matter who we are: basketball coach, priest, or business owner. Whether we are a student or teacher, a husband or wife, mother or father—and as we've just seen—even if you are the Son of God. When you decide to take on the Christian life you will be faced with trials and hardships, and you will be asked to carry your own personal cross on your way to eternal life. From the lips of Saint John Vianney, "You must accept your cross; if you bear it courageously, it will carry you to heaven."[3]

Just like the newly married couple, the confident college athlete, and the success-hungry corporate youngster all didn't realize the challenges and trials they would soon face on their new journeys. So too, I had no idea that soon after I had finally began to enthusiastically practice my faith, I would face the biggest trial of my life. I was completely unaware that so quickly after my full commitment to the focused Christian life, I would be led into my own spiritual desert—not for forty days, but for five months.

Chapter 9: My Journey into the Desert

March of 2015, wrapping up my third year as a part-time assistant basketball coach and preparing for my first year as a full-time assistant. I recall this being the time I became fully focused and truly excited about my faith—when Jesus had become more than just someone I thought about on Sundays and talked to briefly before I went to bed. This was the time in my life when my Christian enthusiasm took off, the time where I felt like I was closer than I had ever been to Jesus and that everything was headed in the direction I had always dreamed of.

Coaching is no different than any other profession. In that, when you first get into the business you start to dream about all the great things that are going to happen in your career. Just like so many other coaches, I began to dream about the championships I would win, the places I would go, people I would influence, and history I would make. Just like most young coaches, I had a plan for how my career was going to play out, step by step. I was ready to take the coaching world by storm—and how hard could it be anyway? I was an assistant coach for a successful basketball program, working for a veteran head coach, who just so happened to be my Father. There was no doubt in my mind I was set up for success—and with my newly established spiritual life and Jesus on my side, nothing could stop this coaching freight train from reaching its planned destination. I remember telling my Dad several times, half-jokingly and half-seriously, "Ok, Dad, here is the plan. You are going to coach for ten more years, we are going to win a lot of games, and then when you retire I'll take over for you and become the head coach at my alma mater, in my home town, and continue what we started here." With a smile and shrug he would always respond with the chuckling response, "Sounds good to me!"

So the plan was set. I knew exactly where I was going to be for the next 20-30 years, my family and I would be financially comfortable, we would be living where we always had wanted to, and we'd have the life we had always planned on having. Things were going perfectly according to my well thought out plan. I had an amazing wife and son, a new house, a great job doing what I loved, at a place that I loved—things couldn't get any better than this.

After another successful but long and tiresome basketball season ended, the time to relax and recharge my coaching batteries had finally come. So we all made our way up to Wisconsin over the Easter weekend to be with our extended family. A few days into our trip my Dad, and at the time my current boss/employer, received a phone call and was offered an assistant coaching position at the University of Virginia. When he told me what the phone call was about, in my selfishness, my heart sank in fear and worry. After putting on a happy face for my Dad for such an amazing opportunity, I asked if he was going to take the job. Although at the time he told me he wasn't sure what he was going to do, deep down I already knew the answer.

As we made the long drive home from Wisconsin to Missouri the reality of the situation began to take over my thoughts. "If and when Dad takes this job, I will no longer have a job. What will I do for money, where will I coach, how will we pay for our mortgage?" As the uncertainty began to grow in my mind, so did my fear and anxiety. During that six hour drive home with my head on the seat in front of me, tears quietly fell from my eyes. I don't know if I prayed in fear or in anger. I'm not sure if I prayed for guidance or for help. I'm not sure what I prayed for during that long drive home. All I remember is that I prayed, long and hard, I prayed.

Within about one month's time everything I had been fearing had come to fruition. My Dad took the job at Virginia and the coach who was hired to replace my Dad didn't want to hire me. In less than four months, I went from a place of great spiritual strength—believing that nothing could diminish my Christian joy—to a place that had brought on so much fear and worry that I could hardly find a moment to crack a smile.

With fear and trembling I had no choice but to walk into my own spiritual desert where I would be tempted to doubt God's plan, and to abandon my newfound relationship with Christ. Where I would fall into depression and fear. Where I would be tempted to think that Jesus didn't really have my best interest in mind. And so began my long journey into the dark valley that was before me. Little did I know that what I would gain on the journey would change the way I approached my life forever.

Chapter 10: Can Suffering be Good?

If you haven't realized it by now, wake up and smell the lies! A large majority of what our society and our American culture teaches us is wrong. Most of the time when you open a magazine, watch a movie, or listen to the latest billboard hit you are being misled into believing that the norms of our society are the truth. Things have gotten so bad that even when we turn on the news, take notes in a college course, or listen to a popular preacher we have to be on guard for the lies that our society—led by the devil—is leading us to believe in. One of the most popular lies that our culture is teaching us today (and has been teaching us for generations) is that suffering is bad. If I told every person that was in the midst of suffering that what they were going through was good, ninety-nine percent of them would look at me like I was crazy and I would surely receive a couple clenched fists and choice words thrown my direction soon thereafter.

Our society, our culture, our world teaches us that suffering is not a good thing. We are taught that when we are having any pain, struggles, or difficulties that we need to get away from those things as soon as we possibly can.

You are struggling in school? The professors aren't helping you learn, you don't think you can make grades? Probably should just drop out, college must not be for you. You didn't make the starting lineup of your sports team? Your coach is hard on you and keeps correcting the mistakes you make? It is probably best that you transfer because the coach has it out for you anyway. Your marriage is struggling? You and your wife are having difficulty getting along? You just don't love your husband the way you used to? Jump ship! No reason to go through that kind of struggle, just get a divorce. Your mother is suffering from terminal illness? She is in great pain? She is miserable lying in that hospital bed? Well, it would probably be best just to euthanize her. It is the merciful thing to do, just relieve her of her pain. You became pregnant unexpectedly? This is a bad time to have a baby? You can't afford a child? A kid will mess up all the plans you have for the future? Having a baby now is too inconvenient for you? Why put yourself through that kind of hardship? Just have an abortion. Get rid of the baby. It is your body anyway and you should decide what to do with your body. This is the world that we live in. This is what people think and this is what people do.

Now many people don't have a choice in these matters. Like the woman who divorces her abusive husband to protect herself and her children or the pregnant teenager who was bullied and pressured into getting an abortion. To those who have no other choice—cling to the Lord and trust in His plan.

That being said, many do have a choice. The choice to accept the trial, unite it to Christ, and become better or the choice to end the struggle, to run away, to abandon ship. Our culture has been and continues to teach us to believe that suffering is bad. Matthew Kelly summed up our cultures understanding of suffering when he wrote, "The world cannot make sense of suffering because it views suffering as worthless. The world has no answer for the inescapable, unavoidable, and inevitable suffering of our lives. Jesus has an answer for everything."[4] Our culture, or should I say the devil, is pulling us away from one of the greatest truths of our Christian faith. A truth that makes no sense to those of this world, but a truth that is none the less life changing—suffering is so good!

"Consider it all joy, my brothers, when you encounter various trials, for you know that testing of your faith produces perseverance" (James 1:2-3). "Not only that, but we even boast of our afflictions, knowing that affliction produces endurance, and endurance, proven character, and proven character, hope" (Romans 5:3-4). "Beloved, do not be surprised that a trial by fire is occurring among you, as if something strange were happening to you. But rejoice to the extent that you share in the sufferings of Christ, so that when His glory is revealed you may also rejoice exultantly" (1 Peter 4:12-13).

There it is my brothers and sisters no mixed words. Saint Peter, Saint Paul, and Saint James all said in their own words that suffering is a good thing. Saint James tells us to *consider it all joy when we face trials.* Saint Paul tells us that we should *boast in our afflictions.* And Saint Peter says that we should never be surprised that we face trials but should *rejoice exultantly in our suffering.*

What does the world think of these words? Does our American culture teach us this? Do our societal norms align with the words of these three great Saints? Obviously not. But I hope most of us have learned by now that the things that the world says are good, usually aren't so good after all. I hope most of us have come to an understanding that the path that our culture is telling us to take, isn't the path that is best for us. The way of the world, is not God's way. The norms of our culture, are not Christian norms. The things that our society teaches, are not the things that Jesus teaches. "For as the heavens are higher than the earth, so are my ways higher than your ways, my thoughts higher than your thoughts" (Isaiah 55:9). The way God thinks isn't the way humans think—and the words that these three Saints, inspired by the Holy Spirit, spoke don't make sense to the world. But for us Christians who have had the pleasure of enduring a cross, it makes perfect sense. We know that suffering brings about growth, trust, understanding, and wisdom—so long as we unite our sufferings to Christ. In the wise words of Timothy Keller, "Suffering will either darken your heart or make you wise, but it will not leave you where you are."[5]

Chapter 11: I am a Leper

Three months had passed since my Dad had taken his new job and I had consequently lost my job. I had spent every waking moment after becoming unemployed trying to fix my problem. I sent in more resumes than I could count, made more phone calls than I can remember. I called in favors, asked for advice, did everything I could possibly think of to find myself a job. My Dad made calls on my behalf to every coach he knew, but none of our efforts were leading to the coaching job I so desired. I finally reached a point where I had basically given up. My wife was doing her best to support us with her minimum wage job and I became a "stay at home dad," babysitting my son, while continuing to search for a coaching opportunity. Those days spent with a one year old, who couldn't talk, gave me many long hours alone with my thoughts. Only when I finally began to realize that all my efforts were doing me no good did I start to write in a journal. During a time of great uncertainty and despair I began to put all my feelings down on paper:

> *August 5, 2015*
>
> *Mark 1:40-41 "A leper came to him, and kneeling down, begged him and said, 'If you wish, you can make me clean.' Moved with pity, he stretched out his hand, touched him, and said to him, 'I do will it. Be made clean.'"*
>
> *I've heard this story 100s of times but for the first time I've made a connection with it. I have related to the leper. I am a leper! I have finally reached an understanding that I am powerless. No matter my efforts I can't find a job. No matter the help I receive from friends/family I still can't find employment. I have been humbled beyond*

measure, because I used to be self-reliant. I used to want to take care of everything on my own, handle every problem, dispel every issue. It took a time when I couldn't, no matter how hard I try, fix my problem, for me to realize I can do nothing on my own. I am no longer self-reliant I am now CHRIST-RELIANT. I come before you Jesus just as the leper, kneeling down I beg you, if you will it, Lord, you can find me a job. If you will it, you can allow me to support my family. Just as the leper, I trust and believe that you are my only hope. Have pity on me. I surrender myself to you. Take care of everything.

Before I was taken into my desert of joblessness, before I was stricken by the realization that I could do nothing on my own, I was your typical over confident youth. I thought I had all the answers and that I could take care of anything thrown my way without any help. After almost three months of not being able to find a job, I started to write in a journal, and only after doing so did I finally come to the realization that I was incapable of making it through this desert without Jesus.

As I was writing this book and reminiscing on this time in my life, I decided to go back and look at all those resumes I sent to countless universities and coaches in hopes of landing a job. To my dismay the main character traits that I used in my profile summary were: "Self-sufficient, Self-starter, Self-driven." It took a time of complete helplessness to make me realize that I was not at all self-sufficient, that I could not handle things on my own, and that when left to my own devices I was incapable of getting the coaching job that I so badly wanted. On this day in early August of 2015, I finally related to a Bible story that I had heard hundreds of times before. Prior to that day I had never paid attention to or connected with the deeper lesson of that story. I finally realized that I was a leper. That I had the disease of pride, self-reliance, and lacked true dependency on God.

In biblical times there was no cure for leprosy, those who acquired the disease were sent outside the city with no hope of ever returning to their normal life. In this account, we see that the leper's only hope was Jesus. This leper came to Jesus desperate, aware that he had no chance of receiving healing by his own efforts, or from the devices of the world. He came to Jesus in complete desperation and complete dependence on His divine healing powers.

Not only in the lepers do we see this complete and utter desperation and dependence on Jesus, but in all the people who come to Jesus for help. All those who came to Jesus to be cured have one thing in common—they all have no one else to turn to. They have all run out of any other options to be cured. Jesus is their only hope. We see this great desperation out of the crippled man whose friends lowered him through the roof (Luke 5:17-26). Or in the helplessness of the man who had been ill for thirty-eight years and had no one to put him in the pool to be healed (John 5:5-9). We see this in the woman who suffered from hemorrhages for twelve years, and as scripture says, "She had suffered greatly at the hands of many doctors and had spent all that she had. Yet she was not helped but only grew worse." This woman of great faith, used up all of her human resources to find healing, finally turns to the only hope she has left: "If I but touch his clothes, I shall be cured" (Mark 5:25-34).

The thing all of these people have in common is first, their initial awareness of their inadequacy and inability to fix the problem on their own. And secondly, their final realization that no human means will cure them of their affliction and that Jesus is their only hope. Complete and utter dependence on God is the virtue that all these people have gained through their suffering.

Why is suffering so good, you ask? Suffering helps us to become aware of our complete and total dependence on God.

Very few people are able to come to a complete understanding of how much they need God by just pondering over the idea. Most people need an experience of complete helplessness to get them there. Anyone will tell you that the greatest way to grow in knowledge and wisdom is through experience. Some of us may need a small amount of suffering to make us fully dependent on God. Others may need their world rocked in unfathomable ways. However, the purpose of all suffering is the same—that we become aware of our inadequacies without God, and realize that Jesus is our only hope. Fulton Sheen said it best when he wrote, "Contentment is based on the idea that 'our sufficiency is not from ourselves but from God.'"[6]

God loves us more than we could ever fathom, and because God loves us He desires what is best for us. And God, being God, knows that what is best for us is that we become fully dependent on him for everything in our life. Whether God causes your trial to occur or He doesn't prevent it from happening, you can be assured that if you unite your sufferings to Christ you will benefit from it. Saint Mother Teresa once said, "Our sufferings are God's gentle caresses beckoning us to come back to Him, to admit we are not in control of our own lives, but He is in control and can be trusted with our lives completely."[7]

Why is suffering so good? Because it makes us aware of how powerless we actually are, it allows us to come to realize how powerful God really is, it forces us to trust and depend on God more fully, and it shows us how much God truly loves and cares for us.

Chapter 12: Fight the Fear

The most common phrase in the Bible relates to one thing—fear. In the New Testament the most common phrase is, "Do not be afraid." In the Old Testament the most common phrase is, "Be not afraid." Do we think this is a coincidence? Do you think that God is trying to get something across to us? God knows that the greatest hindrance of human beings becoming their best is fear. Anthony De Mello wrote, "There is only one evil in the world, fear...and there's not a single evil in the world that you cannot trace to fear."[8]

August 6, 2015

Today has been rough. The burdens of this life are weighing me down. I see no resolution to my job crisis and a part of me wonders if I'll ever get to coach again. But as always Jesus never ceases to amaze me. I sit down for my quiet prayer time while Krayton [my son] is napping, open up my daily devotional and find on the August 6th page: "When things seem to be going all wrong, stop and affirm your trust in me. Calmly bring these matters to me, and leave them in my capable hands."[9]

Oh, how awesome my God is! How reassuring, how kind, how loving Jesus truly is! I can't wait to see Him, I can't wait to hug Him for the first time. And, oh my, how I can't wait to be in His presence for all eternity. What a feeling that will be.

Funny how quickly I lost track of His presence, lost touch with His love. I challenged myself to try to be aware of Him always and less than 2 days later, I can barely get out of bed because of my fear, worries, and burdens. I'm so human, so flawed, and so weak. But what a blessing it is to have a friend like Jesus who will always be there to comfort me no matter how many times I fail, or how many times I lose sight of His love. I feel at peace, I don't know how long my flawed human self will allow this peace to last. But, the comfort of always having Jesus with me is so reassuring. Even though my mind may wander and question, my heart has no doubt, no fear. Because I know my God is faithful, I know Jesus loves me.

Mark 4:37-40: "A violent squall came up and waves were breaking over the boat, so that it was already filling up. Jesus was in the stern, asleep on a cushion. They woke Him and said to Him, 'Teacher, do you not care that we are perishing?' He woke up, rebuked the wind, and said to the sea, 'Quiet, be still!' The wind ceased and there was a great calm. Then He asked them, 'Why are you terrified? Do you not yet have faith?'"

My boat has been caught in a violent storm. I am so much like the disciples. Scared out of my mind. And there is no question that I have asked Jesus the same question the disciples did: 'Don't you care that I'm perishing?' I think Jesus is asking me today the very question He asked His friends back then: 'Why are you terrified? Do you not yet have faith?' It is so easy to say you have faith. If someone asks me if I believe in Jesus, I say yes immediately with confidence and pride. However, it is not easy to live out that faith (especially during times of great stress/worry). I believe in my heart that Jesus loves me, that He is taking care of me, and that He has a plan for me. But just like Jesus' disciples, my head often gets in the way of my heart.

Yes, today my boat is caught in a storm, and today I asked Jesus, "Don't you care?" My mind is terrified of the future and what may come tomorrow. But my heart, and my dear friend, my Lord and Savior, are telling me don't be afraid and just have faith. I know in my heart and so trust my friend to come and rebuke the storm that is before me by saying, "Quiet, be still!" Jesus, I surrender my life to you. Take care of everything.

Can you imagine the fear and anxiety the disciples were feeling as the storm threw around their small fishing boat? You can imagine the thoughts that arose in their minds about what might happen to them. "Will our boat capsize? How will we get out of this? What will happen to our families if we die?" This is what sufferings and trials do. They bring about fear and anxiety. They create worries and uncertainties of the future. The problem that the apostles had was the same issue I had, and the same problem that most of us have when faced with great uncertainty in our lives—we forget that Jesus is in the boat with us! Jesus is right there next to us, well aware of everything that is going on in our lives and completely capable of handling all that we are facing.

Just like the disciples, as I faced the storm that was happening in my life, I lost focus of Jesus and gave all my attention to the storm. In the wake of my storm, looking into the future of uncertainty, I couldn't help but become fearful and anxious. All that was needed to prevent that fear was to refocus my mind on Jesus. All I needed to do was remind myself of His promises, His faithfulness, and understand that although I was facing a storm of great magnitude, Jesus was in the boat with me—and if that is the case there was nothing to fear.

August 7, 2015

I am in search of peace. Not outward peace because that will never be...at least not until heaven. But I desire inward peace. Peace of mind, heart, soul, and spirit. Today's devotional: "Understanding will never bring you peace. That's why I have instructed you to trust in me, not in your own understanding."[10]

This is where I falter. I turn so often to my own mind, my own understanding. By allowing my mind to try to figure things out I go from Christ-reliant back to self-reliant. And when I do this, all I find is fear, worry, anxieties, and depression. All it takes to find peace is a constant awareness of all that Jesus promises me.

All of us, at some point in our lives, will be faced with trial, adversity, pain, and suffering. And for all of us, those struggles will bring out fears and anxieties that will be hard to control because of the uncertainty that so often comes with those difficult times. During those times of uncertainty we must learn to keep our eyes fixed on Jesus, not on our circumstances. If we are constantly living in fear, and are constantly anxious about this, that, and the other—we are making a very definitive statement about ourselves: "...and so one who fears is not yet perfect in love" (1 John 4:18).

If and when you come face to face with suffering, trial, or adversity, an understanding and belief in three simple truths will dispel all the fear and anxiety that you feel. The three truths that drive out fear are:

1. God Is Real
2. God Loves You
3. God has Your Best Interest In Mind

After reading through this list of the three simple truths, can you say that you believe in each of these wholeheartedly? It is easy to say these things are true when you are in the midst of calm in your life. But what if I asked you during an extremely hard time in your life if you thought these three things were true? What if your boyfriend or girlfriend just broke up with you? What if you just lost your job? What if you were just diagnosed with cancer? What if a member of your family just passed away? Having to answer these three questions during a trial makes saying "yes" far more difficult.

In scripture we read, "In the beginning was the Word, and the Word was with God, and the Word was God" (John 1:1-2). For all eternity God was, is, and will be. *God is real!* We are told, "But God proves his love for us in that while we were still sinners Christ died for us" (Romans 5:8). In God's desire that we could be saved and that we could have the opportunity to inherit eternal life, God humbled himself, became man, and died for our sins. *God loves you!* Listen to God as he speaks to you, "For I know well the plans I have in mind for you, says the Lord, plans for your welfare and not for woe, so as to give you a future of hope" (Jeremiah 29:11-14). A perfect plan has been mapped out for each one of us, a plan that is only for our good, and a plan that is designed to give us a 'future of hope.' *God has your best interest in mind!*

When you come face to face with a storm in your life, reaffirm your complete belief in these three simple truths. You may be facing a great trial as you read this book, or your trial may be right around the corner. Whether that time of trial for you is here and now or if you are unaware of when you will face your next trial—whenever you find yourself in the midst of your storm, don't focus your attention on the waves, focus on Jesus. Remember that Jesus is in the boat with you. When the storm comes remember and believe that God is real, God loves you, and God has your best interest in mind.

August 14, 2015

I have finally gotten an opportunity at a job and have a phone interview on Monday. I hope the Lord has prepared me to go into this interview with great confidence. I also hope that I have become strong enough in my faith to accept whatever the outcome is with thanksgiving and gratitude. I still find myself caught up in worries and fears. I still have anxieties about my inability (up to this point) to be able to support my family. However, the closeness I feel with Jesus is so different from where I used to be. I don't always feel at peace, but I am at peace far more often because of the strengthening in my relationship with Christ.

I know leaving Lindenwood [my previous job] is a part of God's perfect plan, which I believe with all my heart will lead to happenings that I could never dream of. It has already led to two things that would not have happened without this change: more time with my family and especially with Krayton, time I would have never had as a basketball coach. And most importantly, and the main reason I believe this happened, my growth spiritually. My faith needed to be tested. I needed to be humbled. I needed to understand what having nothing but Jesus really meant. I needed to fully surrender to the Lord. Thank you Jesus, for your plan, for my suffering.

Chapter 13: The Christian Paradox

Only after I had made the decision to surrender my life completely over to God did my feelings of anxiety, fear, depression, and worry finally began to drift away. I had said the words many times before, "Jesus, I surrender myself to You," but I had yet to fully grasp the enormity of what those words actually meant—that is, giving up any and all control of my life. Allowing God to decide what is best for me, humbling myself to enough to understand that I didn't know what was best for my life. "That is the beginning of spirituality, recognizing the need for God in our lives, and placing ourselves in His hands with complete trust, confident of the tenderness of our Father's love for us."[11] What is the Christian Paradox? *Only by full surrender will you ever become free.*

Again, in the context of the world and in the eyes of our American culture this statement makes no sense. How can I be free if I am not in control? Author, Dale Ahlquist, brings to light our cultures misguided ideas about freedom in his book, *All Roads*, when he stated, "The world insists on misunderstanding liberty. It thinks freedom means disobedience. But it is the opposite. It means obedience."[12] We are taught in our society that freedom means you get to choose to do whatever you want to do. You decide what you do with your body, how you should act, what to do with your talents and resources—and you decide what is best for your life.

But how does this Christian Paradox even makes sense? Many would ask, "Why do I need to become free? I am not a slave to anyone. I live in a free country. How can I be a slave if I am free to do whatever I so choose?" Here lies the answer, and it is the same answer that Jesus gave to the Jews and

Gentiles so many centuries ago. We are enslaved by our sins, our worries, our fears, and our concerns. We are enslaved by our plans, our thoughts, our understanding. We are enslaved by the impossibility of making it through this life unscathed by all the evils that will be thrown at us—and the only way to finally become free of all these things that chain us down is by completely surrendering our will to God's. By completely surrendering our life to Him.

Pope Saint John Paul II teaches us, "Freedom consist not in doing what we like, but in having the right to do what we ought."[13] This beautifully profound statement sums up the confusion that our culture has created in our definition of freedom. I'm sure many of you (like me when I first read this quote) are thinking, "thanks for the thoughts JP2, but what does doing what we 'ought' entail? And what in the name of sweet-fanny-Anny does 'ought' mean anyway?" In the dictionary this word is defined as a 'duty or obligation,' and more specifically, a 'moral obligation.' So what does that mean in regards to Saint John Paul II's statement? Freedom means choosing to do what is morally the right thing to do. Ok, so how do we know what is morally the right thing to do? The morally right thing to do is always (every time, in every circumstance, no matter what) what God wants you to do. So what have we concluded from this long winded explanation:

If freedom equals choosing to do what we ought, and doing what we ought equals God's will, then Freedom equals God's Will. If you are into logic and mathematics, then you will understand that this is a perfect example of transitive law:

If A = B, and B = C, then A = C.

Freedom (A) = Doing what we Ought (B) &
Doing what we Ought (B) = God's Will (C)

Then...

Freedom (A) = God's Will (C)

I hope that quick little math and logic lesson didn't send some of you running for the hills. I promise, no more brain busters from here on out. But in all seriousness, this simple formula has helped my spiritual life as much as anything that I have come to learn. When I finally committed to surrendering my life completely over to God is when my spiritual life began to strengthen and enhance. Even now, as I continue to learn to more fully surrender to God's will, the more my spiritual life grows and the closer I get to complete internal freedom and peace. If you desire freedom in this life, surrender your entire life, your entire self, completely over to God. If you want to find peace and contentment—surrender your wants, desires, hopes, dreams, future, finances, health, safety, family, friends, successes and failures, virtues and vices, sins and good works totally over to God. Surrender all that you are and all that you will be to Jesus. Want to be free? Just let go, let God, and enjoy the ride.

August 18, 2015

My devotional today: "Anticipate coming face to face with impossibilities: situations totally beyond your ability to handle. This awareness of your inadequacy is not something you should try to evade. It is precisely where I want you."[14]

I am unsure if I am nearing the end of my confrontation with this jobless situation. Who knows, it may be only the beginning. If I don't get this job I interviewed for yesterday, it surly may be just the start. However, I do know that I have become completely aware of my inability to handle my current situation. God has gifted me with the knowledge that I am inadequate, and I can do nothing, accomplish nothing, and achieve nothing without Jesus' grace, power, and love. I surrender to your will. I surrender my life to you Jesus. Take care of everything. Work through me, on my behalf, as I rest in the shadow of your Almighty presence.

We have two shining examples of how to completely surrender to God's will. The two examples are from the only two humans in the history of the world that were sinless—Jesus and Mary. We see Mary on the night of the annunciation choose to do God's will, allowing the Holy Spirit to 'overshadow' her and conceive a child within her womb. Most people, I think, believe that Mary didn't have a choice in this matter that she was going to become pregnant no matter what she wanted. This is completely untrue! Mary, in her perfect surrender to God and His plan for her, tells the angel Gabriel, "Behold, I am the handmaid of the Lord. *May it be done to me according to your word*" (Luke 1:38).

If we can, for a moment, divert from topic and appreciate what Mary has done for us. Without Mary we have no chance at eternal life. Without Mary's "yes," without her surrender to God's will, we have no Savior. As Catholics, we are often asked by our non-Catholic brothers and sisters why we honor Mary the way we do. That's why! Without our Holy Mother surrendering her life to God's perfect plan, we have no shot at eternal life. Thank you, Mary!

From the womb of the person who made the original perfect surrender came the man who would, thirty-three years later, make the most important surrender to God in all of human history. The night before Jesus was to be crucified we find Him in the garden of Gethsemane, on His knees, in agony, praying to His heavenly Father. In all His divine knowledge Jesus could see and feel the pain that He would soon have to endure while suffering on the cross, and He begged His Father for it all to be taken from Him. In this most beautiful of scenes we see Jesus in all of His humanity. We see His fear, worry, and anxiousness. We see His complete and utter agony, so much so, blood fell from His pores. But during a time when we are witnessing all of Jesus' unrelenting human emotions, we are also witnessing all of Jesus' perfection through His divine spiritual self. "Father, if You are willing, take this cup away from Me; still, *not My will but Yours be done*" (Luke 22:42).

Just as the angel appeared to Jesus in this moment to comfort Him, we all should use this scene to comfort us. For all of us, this scene should be extremely encouraging and uplifting. To see the God of the universe in all His humanity struggle so greatly allows us to be understanding and hopeful in our own struggles and distresses. This scene is telling each and every one of us that it is ok to have moments of worry, and stress while in the midst's of trial and pain. Human nature comes with human feelings and emotions. However, Jesus' example also shows us that our human feelings do not need to pull us away from our trust in God, but should actually draw us closer. In this moment of fear and agony Jesus is tempted to lose faith in His Father's plan. Every aspect of His human intellect and human understanding is telling Him to run from His certain and impending death. However, in His divine perfection, in His perfect spiritual understanding, Jesus surrenders not to His human emotions but surrenders completely to God. Resting not on His human understanding but on His understanding of the Divine truth—His Father is real, His Father loves Him, and His Father's plan is perfect. "Not my will but yours be done."

August 20, 2015

Still no call back about a second interview. I can feel myself slowly drifting into my state of depression. I don't want to speak. I am lost in the fear of the future and the disappointment of not being able to do what I love, or what I am good at. I've prayed all week to be ok no matter the outcome [of the job opportunity], but it is so hard to fight human emotions.

71

Jesus, you know all that is happening and all that will happen. You know my deepest feelings and why I am feeling them. Please take the pain of uncertainty from me. Grace me with your presence. Enter my heart, mind, and soul. Take control of my thoughts, feelings, conscience, and unconscious. Grant me peace based not on my circumstance but on the fact that I'm so loved by You. I want to be joyful no matter what. I want to be at peace at all times. I see the storm approaching my boat.

A year away from coaching will be so difficult. Lord, get in my boat with me. Calm the storm and stop the waves that are violently crashing upon my boat. If that is not your will, Lord, I trust you. Just please stay in the boat with me as I make the long journey through the eye of the storm. My mind may be fearful and troubled. But my spirit is trusting and unafraid. Stay near me Jesus. Grant me your peace.

"When the way before you seems dark and threatening you can still trust me to guide you. Instead of trying to see through the clouds of uncertainty up ahead, fix your eyes on me."[15]

Never allow your human emotions to discourage you. If a struggle or a trial in your life brings you feelings of fear, anxiety, or depression don't become discouraged. All that says about you is that you are a human being. However, just as Jesus found the strength not to give into His human emotions during His trial, so too do you have the divine ability to do the same. As long as you keep your eyes fixed on Jesus and your mind centered on God's faithfulness—no human emotion or worldly struggle can pull you away from Him. Be strengthened, encouraged, and motivated by Jesus. He is the way, the truth, and the life. Use His and His mother's examples of perfect surrender to help you on your quest to surrender your life completely over to God's will.

> *"I am a handmaid of the Lord, let it be done to me according to your word" (Luke 1:38).*

> *"Not my will but yours be done" (Luke 22:42).*

Chapter 14: When you Surrender, you Die!
(Sounds a bit heavy but keep reading)

What does surrendering really mean? If I surrender to God, am I giving up opportunities for fun, excitement, and adventure? I hope, thus far in the book, one thing has been very clear—God loves you! If we know that God loves us, then we know that God desires for us to be happy. God wants us to live a life of great success, adventure, and joy. "If you then, who are wicked, know how to give good gifts to your children, how much more will your heavenly Father give good things to those who ask Him" (Matthew 7:11). Just as all parents desire for their children to find success, happiness, joy, and adventure in their life—so too—God in his profound love for us, desires us to find great happiness in our life.

What we must first understand is that God knows us better than we know ourselves. "Before I formed you in the womb I knew you" (Jeremiah 1:5). "Even all the hairs of your head are counted" (Matthew 10:30). God knows us so well that He knows our desires, hopes, and dreams even more than we know them ourselves. He knows what our goals are at this moment and He knows what our goals will be thirty years from now. What we need to understand is that God's plan for us perfectly aligns with our deepest and most intimate desires, the ones that lie in the depths of our hearts.

Most of us don't really know what we truly desire deep down in the depths of our soul. You may right now, at this stage in your life, desire fame and fortune. You may want to be an actor or an artist. You may desire to be a professional athlete or, like me, dream of being a championship winning college basketball coach. Sometimes the desires that we have perfectly align with God's desires for us, and if that is the case, that is a great thing. BUT, BUT, BUT! Don't forget, sometimes, God's desires for us don't match up with the desires we have at the current moment, and what most people aren't willing to accept is that—that is a great thing, too!

September 3, 2015

My devotional yesterday: "When you depend on me continually your whole perspective changes...you begin each day with joyful expectation, watching to see what I will do."[16]

I think this is part of what the last 4 months have given me. I have become fully aware of my inability to do anything without God. I have been humbled to a point where I now fully depend on Jesus to give me everything I need. Jesus has strengthened our relationship to a point where I love and trust him with all my heart, all my mind, and all my soul. And all of this has made me so excited to see all that God has in store for me and my family. I have no idea what tomorrow holds. I don't know if I'll be coaching this year or if I won't have a job. It doesn't matter. This adventure that my family and I are on is only beginning, but I am so excited to see how it goes. It is like waiting to open up the biggest Christmas present that sits under the tree as a child. You have no idea what is inside the present, but you know it is going to be amazing!

I never want the understanding I have gained over these last four months to go away. No matter how successful (or unsuccessful) I become, I forever want to be aware of my weakness, be humbled by it, love and trust my Lord, Jesus Christ, and wake up every day with a joyful expectation of what God has in store for me. I love you, Jesus!

The great C.S Lewis describes what surrendering really means, "It means unlearning all the self-conceit and self-will that we have been training ourselves into for thousands of years. It means killing part of yourself, undergoing a kind of death."[17] What does surrendering to God mean? It means you die to yourself. "For whoever wishes to save his life will lose it, but whoever loses his life for my sake will find it" (Matthew 16:25). When you decide to give up your own life for God, you will find a life that is more abundant than you could have ever imagined. "Amen, amen, I say to you, unless a grain of wheat falls to the ground and dies, it remains just a grain of wheat; but if it dies, it produces much fruit" (John 12:24).

Until we choose to die to ourselves we will continue to walk through this life not reaping the bountiful harvest that our God so desperately wants to give us. Until we die to our own wants, hopes, dreams, and desires we won't have a chance to experience the wonderful adventure that God wants to take us on. Matthew Kelly hits the nail on the head when he describes our cultures greatest misconception, "Humanities greatest foolishness is the discredited fantasy that we can find lasting happiness separate from the will of God."[18]

"For if we have grown into union with Him through a death like His, we shall also be united with Him in the resurrection" (Romans 6:5). What does surrendering mean? It means suffering a death like Jesus'. At this point you are probably really starting to think I'm crazy. No, I don't mean that we all should desire to be crucified, scourged, or tortured. What I mean is we have to die, not in the same physical way as Christ but in the same intentionally willing way as Christ. 'A death like His' means a death that we voluntarily concede to, a death that we willingly commit to, a death that we faithfully decide to act out on our own accord. Our dying is not a physical death but a spiritual death. A death in which we crucify our own will, for the sake of God's will. That is what dying to self means.

Chapter 15: Reap the Reward

How can suffering possibly be a good thing? Why should I take up my cross and follow Jesus? Why should I surrender my life or die to myself? How can pain and struggle possibly benefit me? For the last seven chapters all we have talked about are trials, tribulations, suffering, surrendering, and dying. We have focused on the process of giving up our own will, our own desires for the sake of God. Enough is enough, we want to reap the reward! Jesus tells us, "Take My yoke upon you and learn from Me, for I am meek and humble of heart; and you will find rest for yourselves. For My yoke is easy, and My burden light" (Matthew 11:29-30). Frankly, this whole yoke is easy/burden is light talk doesn't connect very well with all the suffering and pain that we have been discussing—and until you experience your own trial and unite yourself to Christ during your sufferings, you won't fully be able to understand how pain and difficultly can be easy or light.

September 10, 2015

A few lines from my devotional the last few days:

"Trust in Me with all your heart and I will make straight your path."[19]

"As I assured Jacob, when he was journeying away from home into unknown places, I am with you and will watch over you wherever you go."[19]

"Let these assurances of My continual presence fill you with joy and peace."[19]

Every time I get to a point where I think I have it figured out or it looks like we know what is going to happen, something comes to make chaos of it. I am so thankful for my growing faith life and my strengthening relationship with Jesus. If this was 6-8 months ago, I don't think I could have handled all this uncertainty, all this stress. As of today I am more at peace than I have ever been. I fear nothing, I worry not about the future and become anxious, not about my life or my family's life. I am so confident in God's plan for us and in His unfailing love, that when all of these earthly concerns present themselves, all I tend to think of are my heavenly concerns. This confidence and peace is surely bound to sway, because I am only human, but knowing this feeling and knowing this type of trust and love brings me more joy and more peace than I ever could have imagined.

We need to learn to recognize our sufferings and our struggles not at burdens but as gentle nudges from God, lovingly pushing us towards complete surrender to him. Through our trials and our failures God is quietly reminding us that we can do nothing on our own, that without him we are helpless. Through our fears, depressions, and anxieties God is drawing us closer and closer to him so that we may finally realize that the peace, comfort, and contentment that we all desire resides only in his holy arms. For some it may be through homelessness, sickness, or joblessness. For others it may be through death, divorce, or betrayal. Whatever your trial may be, God is using it to open your eyes to what you really need and what really matters. No matter what your struggle is right now, no matter what your struggle may be in the future, if you unite your sufferings to Christ you will see your faith take off into stratospheres that you never could have dreamed of.

If through your trial you learn to surrender yourself to Christ, you will come to trust Jesus more than you ever could have imagined was possible. If by way of your own cross, you die to yourself for the sake of Christ, you will find more peace, joy, and thankfulness than would have ever been possible without it. This trial that you are facing now or the one you will face in the future was/will be given to you by God for a reason. For through your affliction you will find endurance, wisdom, and trust. Through your suffering you will find faith, hope, and love. Through your pain you will come to realize, just as the leper, that Jesus is your only hope—and trust me, Jesus' plan is always better than our own.

September 23, 2015

After 5 months of uncertainty, struggles, worries, and stress, I have officially been offered a full time coaching position!! Praise my God, my Lord, and my Savior, Jesus Christ!! How faithful You are to your children, how caring and loving You are. Not once did You abandon or forsake me. Not once did You forget of me or leave me to fend for myself. You are my greatest love, my best friend, oh Jesus. You are my constant companion, my gentle guide, my faithful Savior. To You I offer everything! Into Your hands I give You my life, my family, our future, our well-being. Protect us, guide us, and lead us wherever You will us to be. We will follow You with unfailing trust.

Thank You, Lord, for all of Your blessings, for all of my struggles, for strengthening my faith and growing our relationship. Lord, as I begin a new adventure completely guided by You, help me to never forget these last five months. No matter if my road leads to great success or great disappointment. Help me to always remember that without You I can do nothing, achieve nothing, or become nothing. But with You and through You all things are possible. Give me the platform to glorify Your name, tell my story, and preach the good news to all. Thank You, Jesus for Your love, Your faithfulness, and Your friendship. O Jesus, I surrender my life to You. Take care of everything! GOD IS GOOD!

If you are a college basketball coach, you understand how miraculous getting this job actually was. In the college basketball world most job openings come available between the months of March and June. For a job to open in late September, for that job to be close to home, for it to be a full-time position, and provide enough financially for my family can only be explained by God's divine providence.

Although these five months were a tremendous challenge and trial in my life, my struggle doesn't even come close to comparing to what so many people in this world are facing on a daily basis. The loss of loved ones, the trials of terminal illness, the difficulties of homelessness and starvation. The pains of mental, physical, or sexual abuse—the list is endless of sufferings that are far greater than what I experienced in the summer of 2015. However, the cross of unemployment that I had to carry (although minuscule compared to the trials of so many) was the personal cross I was given, meant to draw me into a greater relationship with Jesus. This trial was meant to draw me into a greater understanding of what being a disciple of Christ actually meant, a greater trust in God, and a greater awareness of His goodness and His love for me.

Whether you are asked to carry a small cross or a large one, the purpose of the cross remains the same: To bring you into a closer relationship with Christ, and to awaken you to the true call of the Christian life—*utter dependence of and complete surrender to God.*

3rd Quarter: The Truth

Chapter 16: Life-Long Research Project

Looking back now, those five months in the summer of 2015 were the most important months of my life. While walking through my own personal spiritual desert I truly fell in love with Christ and I learned what trusting in God really meant. I had fallen so in love with Christ that I committed to use every waking second of my life from then on to glorify His name. I desired so badly to please Him, for no other reason than I had come to love Him so profoundly that I wanted to do anything and everything I could that I thought would make Him happy. This feeling was similar to how I felt as I was falling in love with my wife. I would spend hours thinking about ways I could please her or make her smile. I would do extra little things that I knew would brighten her day. I would spend every dollar I had on her. I would use every free minute I had to text her, call her, or spend time with her. I was so in love with my future wife that I yearned with all my heart to do everything in my power to make her happy.

Because of that summer, I learned what trusting in God really meant and gained the confidence to trust that Jesus was always in control—no matter what would come my way. Five months of uncertainty taught me to trust like a little child. Like the child who is so trusting in his parents that no matter what they say, he believes them. Like the child who clings to every word that his father speaks, trusting without a shade of a doubt that what he is saying is true. Like the child on the edge of a diving board whose mother tells him to jump, and though every instinct tells him not to, he jumps anyway—because he trusts his mom to catch him.

This spiritual awakening invigorated me to commit to start taking a real intellectual and mature interest in my faith—this is when the desire to find answers started to enthrall me. I became obsessed with finding out the truth of my Christian faith. Not part of the truth or an abbreviated version. Not just the portions of the truth that I liked or agreed with. I wanted the true blue, down home, 'whole-truth-nothing-but-the-truth-so-help-you-God' kind of truth. I was so in love with Jesus that I desperately wanted to do exactly what He desired for me to do. I trusted Jesus with all my heart, which meant, whatever he said I believed it and was going to attempt to do it.

The origin of Kimberly Hahn's, co-author of *Rome Sweet Home*, Christian beliefs are similar to mine, and similar to so many of us who were raised in Christian homes. "Because I loved my parents, I loved the God they loved. Because I believed my parents, I believed in the God they believed in— that he had done what they said he had done. I believed the Bible was true because they said it was. And yet there comes a time when each of us needs to decide about whether or not Jesus' claims on our lives are, in fact, true."[1]

Whether you are Catholic, Protestant, Muslim, or Atheist, like Kimberly Hahn explains, we should all come to a point in our lives where we decide for ourselves what the truth is. Now unlike Mrs. Hahn, I was raised a Catholic, born into a devout Catholic family, went to a Catholic grade school, was your normal born and bred cradle Catholic. For my whole life I had been told: we go to Church on Sunday, we do the sign of cross after receiving Communion, we confess our sins to a priest, we believe in the teachings of the Church. With holy water in Grandma's bedroom, a rosary on Mom's night stand, and a Mary statue on the mantel—I was your typical do what you're told and don't ask questions kind of Catholic kid. In most cases I had no clue why we did the things we did and I really had no idea what exactly the Church taught, why they taught it, or why I was supposed to believed it. But I was an obedient kid, and even though I was bored or confused most of the time, I did what my parents asked me to do. Because I trusted them and because I loved them.

Although, at this time in my life I had become like a little child towards Jesus, believing everything he said. My innocent child-like trust in my parents had run its course and I was ready to decide for myself what was true. At some stage in every person's life we reach a point where we begin to think for ourselves, where that childish thought of "mom and dad know everything," is gone. At some point we begin to wonder whether or not what we have been told, taught, or come to understand is true or not. Whether it be questions about Santa Clause, where babies come from, or questions about our faith—our individual intellect and curiosity begin to muster up the questions: why, who, how, is that true?

This was the point in my life when I decided (in a spiritual sense) to start thinking for myself. I did not want to continue to be a part of the Church I was raised in just because my Mom and Dad said I should. I didn't want to blindly adhere to all that the Catholic Church taught just because my folks said it was true. I needed to find out for myself. So began my journey to find the truth. I told myself that I was going to approach this journey like a college research project—unbiased, in-depth, and overly detailed. I was committed to learning everything I possibly could about what Jesus wanted, what Jesus said, what Jesus meant, and what the truth that Jesus promised to give me really was. I wanted to know what I had to do to draw myself as close as possible to Christ. I wanted to know what I could do, during my time on this earth, that would make my relationship with Jesus as perfect and as intimate as it could possibly be. I wanted desperately to do everything He asked of me and receive every gift He was offering me. So, through my deep longing and desire for true and perfect intimacy with my Lord and Savior, I began my journey to find the Truth.

Chapter 17: Biased Research

If I am reflecting honestly on the initial approach I had towards my research, I was biased. And not in the way you would think a cradle Catholic would be biased. As I had grown up, gone through college, met new people, and learned new things, my eyes were open to all the different religions (especially Christian religions) that the world had to offer. My best friend was Lutheran, my college teammates were everything from non-believers to Muslims. I had many family members that had left the Catholic Church for other denominations and beamed over their superiority. I had seen videos of non-denominational mega churches. I went to a Baptist church service as a part of my team's community outreach in college. Like most semi-sheltered cradle Catholics, I was surprised and intrigued by all the different churches and all the different ways in which people praised God. I slowly, without even realizing it, became biased against and somewhat resentful of the Church I had grown up in.

I found it pompous and arrogant that my Dad would tell me that the Catholic Church was the original Christian Church. I thought it insensitive of the Church to say that they had the fullness of faith and that the Catholic Church was the Church that Jesus had founded. I found it pretty divisive that the Catholic Church taught that Christian worship was meant to be performed the Catholic way—and that way was the way Christ intended it to be. I questioned, "Why do we need all these rules, all the weird rituals? Why is the Church so strict and old fashioned?" My newfound love and understanding of Jesus made me feel like as long as I love Jesus, who cares how I decide to praise and worship Him.

The more modern and youthful churches intrigued me. The new aged glamour of the churches that housed bands, great musicians, lights, videos, and inspirational preachers started to pull me in. I loved the stories I heard, pictures I saw, videos I watched of Christians crying in praise with hands up as the musicians on staged rocked out a Jesus anthem. I was enthralled by the charismatic preachers I heard on podcasts who would bring crowds of people to their feet in praise by their powerful words. All these things and more made me wonder, "Why does my Church do it the way they are doing it? These other ways seem a whole lot better to me."

As most know-it-all children tend to do, when I started to think I knew more than my parents, I began to test them (my Dad in particular). I began to nag my Dad with all the things I didn't like or understand about the Catholic Church. I would ask him all the tough Catholic questions: "Why does the Church make you go to a priest to confess your sins? Why does the Church teach that a mortal sin separates you from God? Why does the Church hold firm of their teachings of traditional marriage, or oppose sex out of wed-lock? What's with the incense? Why do we pray to the Saints and to Mary so much, why not just pray to Jesus? Why can't we focus more on a good homily that will inspire us and less on the boring preparation for the Eucharist? What about the priest sex scandals? How can we believe a Church that has been responsible for so many horrible happenings throughout history?"

These questions and questions like these are what I would constantly barrage my Father with. In my Dad's wonderful simplicity and steadfast faith he would listen intently to my questioning and arguments and then always respond the same way: "Kramer, I don't know all the answers to your questions, but what I do know is that almost 2000 years ago Jesus told Peter, "you are Peter, and upon this rock I will build my Church, and the gates of the netherworld shall not prevail against it. I will give you the keys to the kingdom of heaven. Whatever you bind on earth shall be bound in heaven; and whatever you loose on earth shall be loosed in heaven" (Matthew 16:18-19). He would go on to say that Peter was the Catholic Church's first pope and that there has been a continual line of successors from Peter until now. "Kramer, I don't know all the answers to your questions, but I do know the Catholic Church has all the answers you're looking for. But, for me, if Jesus said that His Church, the Church He founded, was the Church built on the rock, Peter, and that the gates of Hades will not overthrow it, then I believe Him—and the Catholic Church will be my Church now and forever, not because I have found all the answers or have taken the time to research everything the Church teaches, but because Jesus said it was so." This answer that my Dad gave, although sensible, was incredibly frustrating to me. I didn't want to believe all that the Catholic Church taught just because of one verse in the Bible. I wanted to get specific answers for all the specific questions I had. So off I went, ready to find all the answers my Dad "claimed" the Church had—hoping deep down that I would be able to prove him wrong.

I read books, online articles, any spiritual document I could get my hands on. I watched YouTube videos, movies, documentaries, sermons, homilies, debates, anything that I felt could help me filter out the lies and hone in on the truth. I have spent the last five years completely obsessed with finding out all I could about the Christian faith, about the Catholic Church, and most importantly, about what is true! Walking into this "lifelong" research project (that I am still on today and will never complete in this lifetime), I expected and hoped to find many answers that would prove my Dad's argument to be naive. But after five years of focused, detailed, in-depth research I have yet to find a question that the Catholic Church doesn't have an answer for. I have yet to find a teaching that the Church can't explain. I have yet to find a Catholic tradition that doesn't derive from Christ, the Bible, or the early Church. I set out on this journey hoping to come to the conclusion that I could realize the fullness of spiritual life no matter what Christian Church I attended. But I came to realize that there was only one Church, the Catholic Church, that offered all of the glorious spiritual gifts and graces that God wants to give me.

To my surprise, the research project that I suspected would lead me away from my Catholic faith, actually pulled me closer. My research allowed me to understand more fully the beauty of the Church that Christ founded nearly 2000 years ago. It helped me fall deeply in love with the Catholic Church and all of her history, traditions, doctrines, and teachings. There isn't enough space in a massive library, let alone one quarter of this 160 some-odd-page book, to fully sum up the beauty and truth of the Catholic faith. But for the remainder of this quarter of the book I will present some of the truths I have come across over the last five years that were most impactful to me.

Chapter 18: The Bread of Life

Picture for a moment a fictional situation to help me make the most important, fascinating, intriguing argument for the Catholic Church:

> *True Faith Christian Church is a vibrant faith community. They have a caring pastor, invested church members, wonderful resources, and a strong set of core beliefs that most stout Christians would be happy to abide by. However, recently there has been a steady decline in members, mainly because True Faith Church doesn't offer the new and more modern amenities that other church's do. Their pastor is a little older and in the opinions of many church goers, "his sermons don't seem to be in touch with the culture" and he refuses to soften on his core beliefs that many members say, "almost all normal Americans don't follow." And to make matters worse, two of the pastor's chief advisors were recently convicted in a terrible scandal that happened inside the walls of the Church.*
>
> *Just when the pastor thought all hope was lost and that his Church would fold because of rapidly declining membership, an amazing thing happened—Jesus appeared to him. Now this wasn't a dream or a vision, this wasn't a ghost or an apparition, this was the true flesh and blood Jesus standing before the humble pastor. After seeing Jesus, the pastor mimicked the same sensory judgement that doubting Thomas once did, touching Jesus' hands and side making sure that what he was seeing was really Jesus. In awe and wonder the pastor asked Jesus why He was there. In reply Jesus said, "I*

am here to help grow your Church, to bring members back so that you can help them on their journey towards Me and towards eternal life." Not understanding how Jesus was going to help him do that, he asked plainly, what Jesus wanted him to do. Jesus replied, "Make 500 fliers and put them all around town, rent out a section of the newspaper and write this on all the advertisements:"

THIS SUNDAY...

@ True Faith Church (10am)

JESUS CHRIST WILL BE THERE

(Not his spirit, not his image)

JESUS, IN THE FLESH

Come and touch the living God...

With faith and obedience the pastor did as he was told. He made the fliers, put them up all over town, and started to spread the word. Most people laughed at him, shook their heads, or thought he was crazy. Some figured it was just a desperate ploy to try to get more people to come to his Church. But some people were intrigued enough that they decided they would go on Sunday and see what this crazy pastor was talking about. Maybe, at the very least, he had a cool life-size cardboard cutout of Jesus for everyone to take home with them.

Sunday arrived and pretty much the same members who always came were filing in. A few new faces that the pastor had spoken with showed up as well, not really expecting to see anything more than a normal Church service. When the service started everyone was expecting the typical routine—but instead the *pastor came out on stage and told the congregation that he had someone to introduce to them and pointing back stage out came a tall Middle Eastern looking man with long hair and a neatly trimmed beard. He had on a white robe with a purple sash and sandals on his feet. When the Church goers saw this man they all laughed amongst themselves, thinking this was a Church version of a dress up Santa. However, as the man begin to talk, their hearts burned, and when their eyes met His something inside of them erupted. As the man spoke words of encouragement to them, they all began to realize that this was really Him! This was truly Jesus Christ in their midst!*

In ecstasy and amazement people began to come up to Jesus desiring to be near their Savior. Jesus accepted each of their warm embraces— kisses on the cheeks, timid handshakes, and even some overzealous bear hugs. After the initial shock of the situation was over, Jesus told them that He wanted to spend intimate, one on one time with each of them. So for the next four hours Jesus took the time to talk with each member individually about anything and everything they wanted to discuss. He strengthened each person just by being in their presence. Through this extremely intimate encounter, each person felt like they had received personal grace from Jesus and were ready to face the cruel world and anything that it had to throw at them. After Jesus had spoken with everyone He told them to go on their ways, that He would be back next Sunday, and He also asked them to tell any family and friends who wanted to meet Him to come next week.

After that Sunday, you can imagine word began to spread quickly that the pastor wasn't joking. *The real Jesus was actually at the Sunday service, just like the pastor had claimed. After the television and news stations picked up the story, things began to get quite hectic. Hotels filled up in record time. The parking lot of the Church was full by Friday and people had set up tents in order to be first in line to the Sunday service—where they knew they would to get the opportunity to meet the real Jesus Christ. Record number of people began flowing into the small town. People from miles and miles away, from all different states, and even several people from different countries had made the trip in order to meet Jesus.*

That Sunday, those who had chosen to come were not disappointed. Just as Jesus promised everyone was able to experience the most intimate time with Him. Although there were thousands upon thousands of people at the service, Jesus was somehow able to spread Himself out to everyone—giving them all the time they desired to have with Him. It was almost as if time had stood still and Jesus could be in several places all at once, catering to the personal needs of everyone all at the same time. No one was quite sure how He was able to do this, but no one really cared to understand fully. All the people cared about was the fact that they had an opportunity to spend personal, intimate, one on one time with Jesus Christ, in the flesh.

After that, True Faith Church no longer had any issue with attendance. The pastor didn't change the way he preached, didn't soften on his core beliefs, and the Church didn't add any new technology. People flocked to this Church because they knew the real Jesus was going to be there and that was all that mattered to them. The Church community grew exponentially and the pastor had to build a brand new stadium size Church to fit all of his new members. For those people who had become members and were able to meet Jesus in the flesh, Church service was no longer a drag or a burden. It became something they desperately looked forward to all week. Sunday service was their opportunity to be as close as possible to Jesus, to be strengthened by His real presence, and to be filled with God's grace by simply coming in contact with Jesus' true Body, Blood, Soul and Divinity.

Now let me ask you, if this fictional scenario did really come true one day, what would you do? Would you say it wasn't worth it to go to the service? Would you say that you had too many other things going on or that you needed to sleep in? Would you say that it is nice that Jesus is physically present at that Church but I like the music and the preaching more at the Church I already go to? If this fictional scenario came true, wouldn't you take the time to investigate and actually find out for yourself if what you were hearing was true? If you knew that Jesus Christ, incarnate. Jesus Christ, the word made flesh. Jesus Christ, your Savior and God, was physically present at this Church every Sunday, would you go? At least for those who truly love Jesus, and not just the worldly advantages that come from religion or from a certain Church, it is a no brainer. If Jesus is there, so am I. It is as simple as that.

Now for those of you who don't know where I'm going with this, let me rock your world. The fictional story I just told you has come true. There is a Church that has the real Jesus, in the flesh, at their service every Sunday (and even better, this Church has a service every day, and Jesus is there—every day!). There is only one religious institution in all the world who claims to have the real Jesus present at every Church service. There is only one Christian Church in the world who has the audacity to say that if you come to their service, they will give you the true flesh and blood of Jesus and you will be allowed to intimately connect with Him in a more profound way than you can even imagine. There is only one Church in the entire would who makes the same claim that the fictional pastor of True Faith Christian Church did—and that Church is the Catholic Church! The Catholic Church claims that the bread and wine that they give out at the culmination of every Mass is the true flesh and blood of Jesus, the legit DNA of the divine Son of God, the actual soul and true divinity of Jesus Christ. Let that bold claim sink in for a moment...

So let me ask you a question. Do you think it is worth it to figure out if this claim that the Catholic Church has so boldly made is true or not? And let me state something right here and now. If the Catholic Church is wrong, if the bread and wine that they give out isn't really Jesus and is just normal bread and wine—then the Catholic Church is made up of a bunch of ungodly heretics! The Catholic Church is made up of people who get down on their knees and worship bread and wine. In the words of the great Catholic apologist and former Presbyterian minister, Scott Hahn, "the Catholic Church is not just another denomination—it is either true or diabolical."[2] If the Catholic Church is wrong, who cares where you go to church. It doesn't matter. But, what if what the Church claims is actually true? If the Catholic Church is right, that the bread and wine they give out is the true body, blood, soul, and divinity of Jesus Christ, then what are we doing?

Whether you are a non-Catholic, former Catholic, cradle Catholic, Catholic convert, or a pondering might-want-to-be-a-Catholic-one-day person, we all have to contemplate this information with extreme detail and intensity. If you are the person who doesn't believe a word I just said, or if you say to yourself, "that is impossible, there is no way, that doesn't make any sense," again I ask you—isn't this claim too life changing to approach like choosing which cereal to buy at the grocery store? Matthew Kelly summed up the gravity of what we Catholics believe in a powerful testament in his book, *Rediscover Catholicism*:

> "If Muslims believed that God was truly present in the mosques, and they could receive and consume him in the form of bread and wine, they would crawl over red-hot broken glass for the chance. But as Catholics, we are so unaware of the mystery and the privilege that most of us cannot be bothered to show up to church on Sunday and many of those who do can hardly wait to get out."[3]

If you are someone who has been a member of the Church for your whole life and does believe in the True presence, I ask you this—do you approach Mass in the same way that the members of True Faith Christian Church, in my story, approached meeting Jesus? Do you receive the Eucharist with the same uncontrollable desperation that the Muslims in Matthew Kelly's quote did? If we as Catholics really believe what our Church teaches, why are we skipping Sunday Mass? How can we say Mass is boring? Why aren't we going to daily Mass? Why aren't we adoring Christ in the Eucharist at adoration?

If we really believe what the Catholic Church teaches, then the reverence we show to the Eucharist would be the same we would have shown to Jesus 2000 years ago when He walked the earth—and even more so considering, "None of the people who were cured [by Jesus]—Bartimaeus, or the paralyzed man of Capharnaum, or the lepers—were as close to Christ, to Christ himself, as we are every time we go to Holy Communion."[4]

If we Catholics truly understood what we were receiving every Sunday at Mass, we would all walk down the aisle with tears in our eyes knowing we are about to receive the living God. We would kneel down after receiving communion in exuberant thanksgiving because we know we have just become fully one with Christ. I'll ask it again, if the Catholic Church is right—what are we doing?

Chapter 19: What Jesus Wants

The phrase that I have heard more often in my spiritual studies than any other is, "Being Christian means having a personal relationship with Jesus," or something in that capacity. Whether it be from non-Catholics or Catholics, priests or preachers—I constantly hear that the most important thing we can do in our spiritual life is to create a personal relationship with Jesus. *I believe this is 100% true.* It is the exact same point that I was making in the 1st quarter of the book. If we don't love Jesus, nothing else matters—and it is very hard to love someone if you are not in a relationship with them. Jesus, without a doubt, wants desperately to have a personal relationship with each one of us. But, what most fail to realize is that Jesus wants so much more than just a personal relationship with us. Jesus wants *you* to enter into the most incredibly intimate covenant imaginable with Him.

So let's first discuss what being in a relationship even means? As most of us would be able to explain, being in a relationship means you are connected with another person, that you have involvement or association with someone other than yourself. I can say I'm in a relationship with my next door neighbor. We exchange greetings here and there, lend yard tools to each other when needed, and talk about the big game when we both check the mail at the same time. By definition, that is a relationship. What does being in a personal relationship mean? I would argue that a personal relationship is the same as any relationship, just a little more involved. I can say I'm in a personal relationship with my best friend. I ask for his advice, tell him my struggles, know his likes and dislikes, talk to him all the time. I am in a personal relationship with my best friend.

A covenant, however, is far more than a relationship and even more than a personal relationship. A covenant is a binding of one person to another. A covenant is a gift of complete self, a promise of 100% personal offering and commitment to another. The closest thing we have in human understanding to the covenant that Jesus desires to be in with each of us, is marriage. In marriage, a man and a woman, give themselves entirely to the other. They commit and promise to become one with each other, "til' death do us part." They give all of themselves to the other person through the marital act of sexual intercourse, in which, "the two become one body" (Genesis 1:24). The most intimate of human relationships is the covenant of marriage—and as intimate as this covenant between two humans can be, imagine how much more intimate a covenant like this can be when one of the participants is the divine Son of God.

I can have a relationship with my next door neighbor. I can have a personal relationship with my best friend. But that doesn't mean that either of them want to move in with me, share their entire lives, or offer their entire selves to me.

Jesus doesn't just want to be in a personal relationship with you, He wants to be in a *divine covenant* with you. He wants to create the most intimate relationship that could ever be with you. He desires to be so close to you that our human minds can't even perceive the type of intimacy that He desires. "Then He took the bread, said the blessing, broke it, and gave it to them, saying, 'this is My body, which will be given for you; do this in memory of Me.' And likewise the cup after they had eaten, saying, 'This cup is the *new covenant* in My blood, which will be shed for you'" (Luke 22:19-20). Jesus is establishing and inviting each of us to partake in this 'new covenant' with Him. He is inviting all of His beloved children to continually reestablish their covenant with Him through the breaking of the bread.

Jesus makes it very clear, "I am the living bread that came down from heaven; whoever eats this bread will live forever; and the bread that I will give is My flesh for the life of the world" (John 6:51). Jesus says, "Amen, amen, I say to you, unless you eat the flesh of the Son of Man and drink His blood, you do not have life within you" (John 6:53). Jesus implores us to believe, "For My flesh is true food, and My blood is true drink" (John 6:55). You can hear the desperation that Jesus has for His children, so desiring to be close to them through this perfect mystery, "Whoever eats My flesh and drinks My blood remains in Me and I in him" (John 6:56).

Jesus desires so badly to give you this most intimate gift. Will we be like the many disciples, who murmured saying, "This saying is hard; who can believe it?" (John 6:60) and departed Jesus and no longer accompanied him? Or will we be like Peter and the apostles who when asked if they were going to leave also, responded, "Master, to whom shall we go? You have the words of eternal life" (John 6:68). Like these simple fisherman, we can have the humility to understand that our human minds can't fully comprehend how this mystery works. Like the apostles we can also have the courage to say, "We have come to believe and are convinced that you are the Holy One of God" (John 6:69). And by making that clear and definitive statement, that we believe Jesus to be the Holy One of God, no matter how much our mind tells us something is impossible—if Jesus says it is true, we can believe it. Father John Riccardo's words describing the Catholic Church and the gift of the Eucharist are breathtakingly beautiful and staggeringly true:

> "We are not talking about a club, not talking about a bunch of rules, we are not talking about a code of ethics, or an institution. We are talking about a love story with a person who is crazy in love with you. So much so that He wouldn't just make you, He wouldn't just die for

you, He wouldn't just promise you abundant life but even now every day, if you want to, He unites Himself to you and in you—that's the Gospel."[5]

There is only one Church in the entire would that claims to have Jesus' true flesh for you to eat, and true blood for you to drink—and that Church is the Catholic Church. "The Eucharist is this: not just a beautiful rite, but the most intimate, most concrete, most surprising communion that can be imagined with God."[6] Pope Francis, through his inspired words, describes the union we can have with Jesus in the Eucharist as an almost unfathomably perfect connection to Jesus. Jesus desires not just a personal relationship with you, but the most intimate divine covenant that could possibly be. In the same way a husband and a wife give themselves completely to the other in the marital act—so too, Jesus wants to give Himself entirely to us, so that "two may become one flesh." Jesus desires for us to 'remain in Him and Him in us.' Jesus desperately wants to give His entire self to us so that we can have 'His life within us.' Jesus offers each of us the most perfect gift of all, Himself—and He so desires us to accept this gift for He knows, "the only way that intimate union with Jesus can be fully realized is in the Eucharist."[7]

This declaration that Jesus makes is too significant for us not to try to comprehend. The claim that the Catholic Church makes is too life changing for us not to take the time to find out if it is true. The Eucharist is too perfect a gift for us Catholics to so willing reject it, to so commonly disrespect it, and to so often not appreciate it. Start your journey to find the truth by focusing on the most profound, amazing, wonderful truth of all—that if you so desire, you are able to receive Jesus in the most intimate way you could possibly imagine through the Eucharist given by the Catholic Church.

Why am I Catholic? Short answer...The Eucharist!

Chapter 20: Christianity isn't about Rules

Often I have heard people (mainly current or former Catholics) say that all the Catholic Church talks about are the rules. And if I'm being honest, I must admit, early on in my Catholic revolt I would make the exact same claim. When people tell me now that being a Christian isn't about following rules, it is about loving Jesus and loving your neighbor. I always say, I agree—partially. Saying that Christianity isn't about the rules is like saying that marriage isn't about the rules. That statement is true, marriage isn't about rules. It is about two people falling in love. But just because marriage isn't about rules, doesn't mean there shouldn't be any.

When I married my wife, we were not getting married because of the responsibilities and commitments that would come with it. We got married because we loved one another. However, getting married out of love didn't mean that I wouldn't have some new boundaries that I didn't previously have. Now that I was married, going up to a pretty girl and asking for her number probably wasn't something I should do. Staying out until 4am at the bar with the guys was not really on the table anymore. Now that I was married putting my dishes in the dish washer, putting the toilet seat down, and folding the laundry were some things that I had to try to do a little more diligently than I did when I was single.

I think we can all agree that just because marriage isn't about the rules and only about love, doesn't mean I can go out and have an affair with another woman, not come home at night, or not treat my wife with the respect she deserves. The same is true when you commit yourself to the Catholic Church and become a disciple of Christ. Yes, Christianity isn't about the rules, but just because that statement is true doesn't mean rules don't play an important role in establishing some principles of what it means to be a follower of Christ.

It is interesting to me that we are all completely ok with having rules that govern our country and our states, and rules that manage our roadways. We are just fine with schools and teachers who make rules to keep our children under control in the classroom, and parents have no problem giving their children rules that keep them safe and healthy. But most of us have such a big issue with the Church giving us rules to help keep us spiritually safe and spiritually heathy. Quite a contradiction if you ask me.

The word "rules" from the start puts a very negative connotation on what the Church and Jesus are presenting to their large flock. The saying, "the Church has too many rules," makes it seem like the Catholic Church just came up with a bunch of unimportant laws that you have to check off your list if you want to be in good standing with the Church. Jesus, through the Church, guided by His Holy Spirit, has given us not rules, but loving guidelines that give us the road map to achieving true happiness. It is out of protection, out of divine wisdom, and out of incredible love that Jesus has given the Catholic Church these guidelines in order for them to give to us. The famous definition of love given to us by Saint Thomas Aquinas is, "willing the good of the other." What most people so often fail to realize is that the "rules" that have been established throughout the centuries are truly just our loving Father telling us the things to do that He knows will benefit us and the things not to do that He knows will harm us. It is as simple as that.

The Catholic Church is telling us that if you desire the fullness of Christian faith here on earth, if you want to find perfect spiritual peace and joy, if you want to be as close to Jesus as possible and receive all the wonderful gifts that He wants to give—then follow these guidelines that we have been given by the Holy Spirit, the same guidelines that all the Saints of the Church have followed to help them achieve perfect harmony with God. This is why we hear Jesus say, "If you keep my commandments, you will remain in my love, just as I have kept my Father's commandments and remain in His love" (John 15:10). Jesus doesn't tell us this because He is an egotistical ruler who just wants people to do what He says. He even informs us as to why He wants us to follow His commands, "I have told you this so that My joy may be in you and your joy may be complete" (John 15:11).

This new age Christian idea that being close to Jesus, becoming a strong Christian, and finding lasting joy, can be done anyway we so choose and doesn't require us to follow the rules that Jesus and His Church have given us is extremely misguided. In a marriage certain rules are in place for the betterment of the couple and their relationship. Similarly, the Catholic Church gives us rules (loving guidelines) for the sake of our relationship with Jesus, to keep our relationship strong, to help our relationship continue to grow, and to give us the proper channels to renew our relationship after we do damage to it.

Most of us don't truly desire God to fulfill our spiritual needs, what we really desire are ways for God to fulfill our human needs. We use God for our benefit. We hinder parts of God's will in order to fulfill what works best for us or what is easiest. We take the things we like and ignore the things we don't. We all must understand that a portion of God's law is not God's law. The whole of God's law is perfect. Selecting which part of God's law you want to follow and ignoring the portions you don't is not what Jesus means when he tells us to keep His commands. Summarizing the words of Bishop Robert Barron: "If you claim that Jesus is the Lord of your life, He can't just be Lord over a portion of your life but must be Lord over your entire life. Every aspect, and every facet of your life."[8] If we claim that Jesus is God, then all that God tells us to do should be done—not just those parts that we think are appropriate or fitting for our circumstance.

If you love someone you desire to please them. If you trust someone you take their advice and put that advice into action. When we proclaim ourselves as Christians we are stating two very powerful things: 1.) I love Jesus 2.) I trust Jesus.

When you truly love someone, your love for them doesn't stop after you have proclaimed that you love them. Love is active, love is action. If I say that I love my children but don't put that love into action by providing physical and emotional support—it would be easy to see that I don't really love my children. If I claim to love my wife but don't support her, don't treat her with respect, don't listen to her—it is very obvious that my claimed love for my wife is faulty. The same can be said of our love of Jesus. We can say we love Jesus, but if we don't desire to please Him, don't make an effort to do what makes Him happy—how can we say we really love Him?

In the first quarter of this book we focused on how to love Jesus more completely. I hope, through those chapters you also came to realize how much Jesus loves you. As Father John Ricardo explains, our obedience of Jesus and all He commands of us should not be a get out of Hell free pass but should be a response to His love. Using Father Ricardo's beautiful words for the second time, "Life is supposed to be lived in a response to the love that I've already come to know, opposed to, living in such a way as to get God to love me."[9] If you realize how much you are loved by Jesus, you can't help but love Him back. And if you truly love Jesus, your actions will work to portray that love.

When you truly trust someone, you don't just listen to their words of advice and then go about your life not putting that advice into practice. I can say that I fully trust my Dad, but if he tells me that he doesn't think it is in my best interest to buy that stock and I do it anyway, do I really completely trust my Father? If an athlete claims to truly trust their coach, and their coach tells them exactly what they need to do in the off-season to improve but the athlete decides to do something different, does that athlete really trust their coach? The same can be said about our trust in Jesus. If we claim that we trust Jesus, and He tells us to do certain things and follow certain commands and we decide not to, how can we say that we really trust Jesus?

Christianity isn't about the rules, it's not! Christianity is about Jesus. Christianity is the greatest love story ever told. Christianity is about the God of the universe loving us so much that He gave His only Son so that we may not perish but have eternal life. Christianity is about coming to know this truth and because of this truth learning to love and trust Jesus with all of our mind, heart, soul, and strength. Christianity isn't about the rules. But, if you claim to be a Christian you are also claiming that you love and trust Jesus. If you truly love Jesus, then when He tells you what He wants, you do your best to give Him that very thing. If you truly trust Jesus, then when He gives you advice you act on that advice.

In our lack of love and our lack of trust we have the audacity to claim that the Catholic Church is "all about the rules" and that we don't need to follow their rules to love Jesus. Out of our desire for convenience and ease we have the pride to say that I can love and trust Jesus the way I want and that is good enough. That's not love. That's not trust. If we truly love and trust Jesus, we will make our love for Him and our trust of Him an action and not just a word.

Chapter 21: On this Rock

I hope we can all agree that we don't want to have an inactive love for or an inactive trust of Jesus. We want to put our love and our trust of Jesus into action. We don't want to be two faced in our faith, claiming that we are a Christian but then not loving and trusting Jesus enough to do what He is telling us to do. If you have read this far in the book and not thrown it in the trash, I'd say it is safe to assume that you are committed to trying to do what Jesus is asking of you. But after we make this decision, how do we know that what the Catholic Church tells us to do is actually what Jesus is telling us to do? Couldn't the Church have gotten it wrong? Isn't it possible that these mere humans who are running the Church have made a mistake or a few errors along the way? How do we know that we should do and believe in what the Catholic Church teaches instead of the Lutheran Church, or Baptist Church, or the big mega church down the road, or the 25,000 other Christian Churches that claim to have the fullness of Christ's teachings?

Let's first discuss the answer my Dad so simply gave to me all those years ago. How can we know that the Catholic Church is the Church that Jesus himself founded? The answer to that is very matter of fact, if you believe what Jesus said it is hard to question that the Catholic Church is the Church that Jesus founded. "And so I say to you, you are Peter, and upon this rock I will build My Church, and the gates of the netherworld shall not prevail against it. I will give you the keys to the kingdom of heaven. Whatever you bind of earth shall be bound in heaven; and whatever you loose on earth shall be loosed in heaven" (Matthew 16:18-19). It is as simple today as it was the day my Dad explained it to me and the day Jesus explained it to Peter. If historical evidence proves, and historical experts agree, that Peter was the first pope of the Catholic Church and Jesus literally said that Peter was the one he was going build his Church upon, then unless we don't believe what Jesus said we cannot argue that the Catholic Church is anything but the Church that Christ founded. If Christ himself said that whatever Peter decides to "bind and loose on earth, will be bound and loosed in heaven," then unless we don't believe what Jesus said we cannot argue that the laws Peter laid down for the Church are the laws we should all follow.

Now, let's answer the next protest most people (including myself) have once they come to realize that the Catholic Church is the Church that Jesus founded. How can we be sure the Church hasn't gotten some teaching, or law, or doctrine wrong over the last 2,000 years? How can we know that the Catholic Church hasn't gone off course or taken a path that Jesus never intended? The answer again to that is—if we believe what Jesus said, then we believe what His Church teaches.

The moment before Jesus ascended into heaven He commissioned his apostles with a great task and made a solemn promise to them, "Then Jesus approached and said to them, 'All power in Heaven and on earth has been given to Me. Go, therefore, and make disciples of all nations, baptizing them in the name of the Father, and the Son, and of the Holy Spirit, teaching them to observe all that I have commanded you" (Matthew 28:18-20). First off, this task that Jesus was asking His apostles to accomplish must have seemed impossible, ridiculous almost. How can twelve, sinful, mostly uneducated men evangelize the entire world? Some of them, in that moment, must have thought Jesus was crazy—that just could not be done. But that isn't all that Jesus said, after He presented the apostles with the mission He left them with His promise "And behold, I am with you always, until the end of the age" (Matthew 28:20).

A few things to take away from the last words that Jesus spoke on this earth. First, when Jesus tells His apostles to "make disciples of all nations," do we think he was expecting just twelve men all by themselves to reach every corner of the earth, building churches and guiding millions of people? Of course not. That is why we see the apostles (in historical documents and in the Bible) commissioning other men to shepherd the new flock of Jesus Christ under their tutelage and guidance. We see Peter, Paul, John, etc. all ordaining new bishops, priest, and deacons into the Church so that they can help them with the task of making disciples of all nations. Why does the Catholic Church have a hierarchy of bishops, priests, and deacons all under the care of the Pope? Well, because that is what the apostles were guided to do in order to accomplish the task that Jesus gave to them.

Next, when Jesus tells the apostles to teach all the nations to "observe all that I have commanded you," do we think that everything that Jesus had told His disciples during the three years He was with them was put into the Bible? What so many fail to realize when they claim that they don't need the Church because they have the Bible—is how little of what Jesus said and taught to His apostles was actually written down. "There are also many other things that Jesus did, but if these were to be described individually, I do not think the whole world would contain the books that would be written" (John 21:25). For three years Jesus spent almost every day with His apostles. How many hours of intimate time must they have spent together? Think about all the things Jesus must have taught and explained that He only chose to reveal to them. As John said at the end of his Gospel, it is frankly impossible for every word, every teaching, every plan, expectation, or action that Jesus made to have been written in the Bible. Jesus did not say to the apostles, "teach them to observe all that is commanded in the Bible." Jesus said "teach them to observe all that I have commanded *you*."

This is why being a practicing member of the Catholic Church is such an integral part of being a Christian. If we claim to be a Christian apart from the Church and all that she teaches, then we are separating ourselves from many of the gifts that Jesus desires to give to us. As so many of us cradle Catholics have done, separating ourselves from the Church, we are not only out of line with a lot of what Jesus commands of us—but we are also out of line with what is commanded of us in the Bible. "Therefore, brothers, stand firm and hold fast to the traditions that you were taught, either by an *oral statement* or by a letter of ours" (2 Thessalonians 2:15). "We instruct you, brothers, in the name of our Lord Jesus Christ, to shun any brother who conducts himself in a disorderly way and not according to the *tradition* they received from us" (2 Thessalonians 3:6). "I praise you because you remember me in everything and hold fast to the *traditions,* just as I handed them on to you" (1 Corinthians 11:2). We are told in scripture that we must obey not just what is written in letters, but also what is said through *oral teachings.* We are told in scripture that we must hold fast to the *traditions* that were handed down by the apostles.

I once saw a Facebook post that said, "Tired of the rituals and traditions of the Catholic Church? Come praise Jesus without all the extra baggage!" If we turn our backs on the oral teachings and tradition of the Church, as we just learned, we are turning our back on the Bible and on what Jesus desires for us.

Finally, when Jesus tells His apostles that He is "with them always, until the end of the age," do we think that Jesus meant that He was only going to be with the apostles until the end of their age? Do we think that Jesus forgot that He created Peter,

James, John, Andrew, and the other apostles, mortal men—and that one day they would die? Do we think that after the last apostle died that Jesus was no longer guiding the Church He started and left the new bishops, priests, and deacons to fend for themselves? Of course not! When Jesus said, "I'm with you always, until the end of the age," He was talking to the apostles, yes. But He was also making a promise to all those who would succeed His apostles. He promised to be with His Church—including all future bishops, priests, and deacons—until the "end of the age."

How can we believe that the Catholic Church is the true Church founded by Jesus Christ? Simple! Jesus told Peter he was the rock on which He would build His Church, naming Peter as the first pope of the Catholic Church. How can we believe that the Catholic Church hasn't made any mistakes in their teachings, laws, or doctrines over the last nineteen centuries? Simple! Jesus promised to be with them until the end of the age, and unless we think Jesus could make a mistake, than we can't think that He would allow His Church to.

We cannot allow ourselves to separate, depart, or ignore the most beautiful gift that Jesus has given us. We cannot allow ourselves to be seduced into thinking that we know more than the establishment that Jesus promised to guide until the consummation of the world. We cannot be so prideful to think that we have all the answers or that we can get along just fine outside the foundation and path that Jesus laid to help us get to Heaven. We cannot allow ourselves to be so stubborn as to not see the proof given to us by historical and biblical documentation, the proof that leads us to the truth. The truth that the Catholic Church is the true Church of Jesus Christ and the only place where we all can receive the fullness of the Christian faith as Jesus intended it to be.

Chapter 22: Pillar & Foundation of Truth

No Christian, no matter their denomination will argue that the Bible is not Sacred Scripture, that the Bible isn't the true word of God. What I didn't realize—and I assume others like me don't realize—is that the Bible wasn't given to the apostles by Jesus, it didn't fall from the sky like the manna in the desert. The Bible was a collection of writings arranged, selected, and compiled by none other than the Catholic Church in 382 A.D. at the Council of Rome and later reaffirmed by the regional councils of Hippo (393) and Cartage (397). Anyone who believes the Bible to be sacred scripture, consequently believes that the Catholic Church has the authority to select what writings are sacred and what writings are not. Anyone who believes that the Bible is the true word of God, consequently believes that, "...the Church of the living God," is "the pillar and foundation of truth" (1 Timothy 3:15).

Jesus said, "I am the way, the *truth*, and the life." He came to this earth to set the captives free, to show us all the way to eternal life. For those who, like me, try to hide from the truth, who are selective in what they treat as truth, or who alter the truth for their own interest and ease—we have been fooled by the lies of the devil and temptations of our fallen human nature. Fulton Sheen describes the choice we are all making when we give into this temptation, "They didn't want to be drawn up to Him [Jesus], but to draw Him down to them."[10] Don't hide from the truth, don't avoid the truth because you're worried what you'll find. It takes great faith to pursue truth. In the words of Anthony De Mello, "An openness to truth, no matter the consequences, no matter where it leads you and when you don't even know where it's going to lead you. That's faith. Not belief, but faith. Your beliefs give you a lot of security, but faith is insecurity."[11]

Be open to all that Jesus is offering to you, and if and when the truth leads you to where it led me, be willing to accept the gift that is the Catholic Church—whose desire it is to lift you up to Christ during your time on this earth. Ask and you shall receive, seek and you shall find. Jesus proclaimed to Peter that He would build His Church upon him, the rock. Jesus assured His Church that the gates of hades would not prevail against it. Jesus promised the leaders of His early Church that He would be with them until the end of the age. Jesus did not lie!

From a minuscule and persecuted beginning the Catholic Church has grown into the largest, most powerful organization in all of human history. The Egyptian Empire, the Roman Empire, the Russian Empire, the Ottoman Empire have all risen to power and fallen from power—but the Catholic Church has remained. "Every single day the Catholic Church, feeds, houses, and clothes more people, takes care of more sick people, visits more prisoners, and educates more people than any other institution on the face of the earth could ever hope to...the very essence of health care and caring for the sick emerged through the Church...Almost the entire Western world is educated today because of the Church's pioneering role in universal education...the Catholic Church educates 2.6 million students every day...the Catholic Church has a nonprofit hospital system comprising 637 hospitals, which treat one in five patients in the United States every day."[12] From the scientific method, to the big bang theory (although most don't realize), the Catholic Church has been a leading contributor to the growth of science over the last 2,000 years. In spite of corrupt leaders, and terrible scandals the doctrine has never been tainted. Even in times of great crisis, schism, and division the Church has never ceased to exist.

A human institution cannot possibly accomplish all that the Catholic Church has. A mere man-made, man-run organization cannot withstand the things the Church has over the centuries. That is because the Catholic Church is not a man-made institution or a human-run organization. The Catholic Church is the divinely guided, true Christian Church, founded by Jesus Christ.

The world tells us that truth is relative and subjective. If you believe that the grass is blue and the sky is green, that is your prerogative. The world tells us sex before marriage is ok, that contraception is good, and that abortion is a choice not murder. The watered down Christian world tells us that we don't need to confess our sins to a priest, or go to Mass on Sunday, or receive the sacraments. The world tells us that the Catholic Church is wrong, evil, the "whore of Babylon." We were not made for this world! We must keep our eyes fixed on Jesus and listen to His words—not the words of the world.

"I gave them your word, and the world hated them, because they do not belong to the world any more than I belong to the world. I do not ask that You take them out of the world but that You keep them from the evil one. They do not belong to the world any more than I belong to the world. Consecrate them in the *truth*. Your word is *truth*. As You sent Me into the world, so I sent them into the world. And I consecrate Myself for them, so that they also may be *consecrated in truth*" (John 17:14-19).

Chapter 23: Never Question the Church

I think one of the things that initially had me resenting and slightly protesting the Catholic Church was this idea that, I had come to think, I was not allowed to question the Church. And if a large majority of lay people believe that they can never ask questions in order to help them understand the Church, we have a big problem on our hands. In wake of the recent child abuse scandal, we would be delusional if we didn't question what was happening within our Church. This scandal, in all respects, requires complete condemnation and righteous anger from all the faithful. But it is imperative that we first understand the difference between questioning the Church as a whole and questioning an individual member of the Church.

When I use the word 'question,' in regards to the Church in and of herself, I don't mean to be skeptical or cynical but rather desire to learn and understand. On the other hand, questioning, opposing, or publicly denouncing in a civilized, fully informed, and lovingly Christian way the decisions, words, or actions of individuals within the Church can in many cases be merited—especially in the case of the priest sex scandal. With that being said, we must learn to see Christ in all people even those who have committed grave sins and must also learn to forgive. Rather than reject the Church because of the errors of individual members, we as Catholics should all look to examine ourselves more closely to see if we are living our life up to Christ's standards.

If you find an individual within the Church to have imperfections, made mistakes, or even committed great evil that doesn't mean the Church or Her doctrine is flawed. All it means is that sinful individuals who are a part of the Church have given in to the temptations of the devil and of their fallen human nature. It wouldn't make sense to burn the Declaration of Independence because of the Watergate scandal, to throw out the institution of marriage because of the divorce rates, or to ban the boy scouts or public schools because of their recently uncovered issues with child abuse.

We as a human race are sinful and fallen. Wherever there are humans there will be scandal. Unfortunately, that also means that sin will rear its ugly head within religious institutions, including the Catholic Church. If you judge the Church by looking at the individuals that make it up, you will of course find weakness, sin, and sometimes unthinkable evil. But if you judge the Church by understanding Her doctrine and Her mystery, you will only find purity, virtue, truth, and holiness. In the wise words of one of my trusted advisors and friends, Fr. Michael Giesler stated beautifully, "We must always remember what the Church is in herself: the suffering yet glorious body of Christ—suffering in her sinful members, yet glorious in her sacraments and grace." And in all of our sinfulness we are reminded, "...Christ loved the church and handed Himself over for her to sanctify her, cleansing her by the bath of water with the word, that He might present to Himself the church in splendor, without spot or wrinkle or any such thing, that she might be holy and without blemish" (Ephesians 5:25-27).

Before I understood the difference between an individual within the Church and the Church in and of Herself—I was ready to jump ship. Until I finally decided to separate the two and took the time to intellectually understand the magisterial teachings, the sacred traditions, and the doctrine of the Church—I was uninterested, unappreciative, and frankly somewhat ashamed of being Catholic. Before I personally investigated what the Church believed and took the time to understand why they believed it, I resented and disagreed with a lot of what "I thought" the Catholic Church taught. The famous quote from Fulton Sheen, which should be on the front page of every Catholic book ever written, perfectly sums up this disillusioned disdain that so many of us have against the Church, "There are not over a hundred people in the United States who hate the Roman Catholic Church; there are millions, however, who hate what they wrongly believe to be the Catholic Church."[13]

I disliked what I didn't understand. I scoffed at what I didn't think made sense. I talked down upon what I had never taken the time to investigate. I made the mistake that so many millions of people do. I tried to conform the Church to my thinking, my ideas, and my opinions—and in my arrogance never thought, that maybe just maybe, I didn't know everything and perhaps I was the one who needed to change my thinking, not the Church. Although I had been a part of the Church my whole life, I viewed it from the outside, never before willing to open the giant intellectual doors and walk deep into the bowels of the Church and view it from the inside. Those who stand on the outside of a Church on a sunny day only see a dark and gloomy Church. In a similar way, when I finally committed to walking through the doors and viewed the Church from within, only then, did the sun shine through the stained glass windows and reveal the true beauty and divine glory of the Catholic Church.

Questioning the Church is not a spiritual no-no, it is a spiritual yes-yes! Jesus desires us to use our intellect, understanding, and intelligence. Our bishops, priests, and deacons welcome questions, dialogue, and conversations. The Catholic Church is the only Church in the world who encourages you to ask the tough questions—because the Catholic Church is the only Church who has an answer to every one of them. "The truth is not afraid of your questions. The question is, are you afraid of the truth?"[14] I encourage all of you who are reading this book to begin to think critically about what your Church teaches, no matter what Church that is. I challenge you to take the time to ask the difficult questions and go on an unbiased intellectual journey to find the truth. Take the advice of C.S Lewis, "Once you were a child. Once you knew what inquiry was for. There was a time when you asked questions because you wanted the answers and were glad when you found them. Become a child again: even now."[15]

Questioning the Church in order to understand is a good thing. The problem that most Catholics and non-Catholics have is that they throw out possible truth before investigating it for themselves. You cannot disagree or discard another's stance without first knowing or trying to understand the reasoning behind their particular position. Those of us who have left the Church without taking the time to understand all that she teaches, or those who oppose doctrine, law, or moral teachings without first understanding them, can be compared to a person who questions Isaac Newton's Laws of Gravity without first trying to learn and understand his findings. If you are going to question or rule out something that the Church teaches, first do the research! "Do we actually believe that we know better than the collective towering genius of Catholic philosophers and theologians of the past 2,000 years? How did we become so proud and arrogant that we question these extraordinary men and women without hesitation or investigation?"[16]

Of all us cradle Catholics who have left the Church, not one of us have left for a good reason. That is because there is never a good reason to leave Christ's Church, not one! No one would leave the Catholic Church if they truly knew what they were leaving. You couldn't. The issue that our Church faces is that a huge percentage of Catholics don't actually know what they have. We don't know our faith and intern don't realize what we are leaving. Again, the venerable Fulton Sheen explains the mistake so many of us cradle Catholics make, "However sincere and enthusiastic they were, they were, nevertheless, bent on pulling Divinity down to the level of the human."[17] We desire to conform the Church to what we think it should be. We allow our worldly understanding to become more intriguing and relevant than the Church's spiritual understanding. We want to pull the Church down to our human level and pull it away from Jesus' divine and heavenly level.

In the Biblical story of *The Rejection at Nazareth* (Luke 4:16-30), we see Jesus return to His home town, a place He spent a majority of His life, the place He had grown up. Jesus went into the synagogue and was handed a scroll to read. After hearing Jesus speak, the people of Nazareth were amazed by his words. They began to ask, "Isn't this the son of Joseph?" and because of their lack of faith, they were unable to see any signs. Although amazed by His words and aware of the wonders He had done, the people of Nazareth had come to know Jesus as an ordinary carpenter, making them unwilling to believe He could be the Messiah.

Maybe they wanted something more. Maybe Jesus was too ordinary or too boring for them to believe he was the Son of God. Maybe they assumed that the Messiah would be a powerful Zeus-like god shooting lightning bolts out of his hands. They surely must have said, "This ordinary carpenter cannot be the Messiah that was foretold by the prophets." In their lack of faith, as "they were all filled with fury" (Luke 4:28) towards what they did not understand, the people of Jesus' home town, those who had grown up with Him, "drove Him out of town, and led Him to the brow of the hill on which their town had been built, to hurl Him down headlong" (Luke 4:29).

To all my fellow cradle Catholics, we should all begin to feel very uneasy as we read this passage. Whether we are fallen away cradle Catholics, cafeteria Catholics, or thinking-about-leaving-the-Church Catholics, we have all been with Jesus our entire lives, and we may have grown up thinking the Mass was boring. We may have grown up treating the Eucharist as ordinary. In our misunderstandings we may have become infuriated at some of the Church's teachings. As cradle Catholics we must reflect hard on whether we have become the people from Jesus' home town. That just like those who grew up in Jesus' presence, who didn't realize or appreciate the gift they had been given, we like them—are ready to throw Him off a cliff. We all see our Church full of members who, if they haven't already, could, in the drop of a hat, leave the Catholic Church and the Eucharist (Jesus' true self) because it seems too boring, too ordinary, or too old fashioned. Just like the people of Nazareth who were ready to throw Jesus off a cliff, so too, are many Catholics ready to throw away Jesus in the Eucharist and in His Church because of a lack of understanding, a lack of faith, and a human mind that says, "Isn't this the son of Joseph?"

There is nothing wrong with wanting answers for the teachings of the Church. There is nothing wrong with asking questions that will help you better understand all that the Church stands for. That is good, that is holy, and that will lead you to the truth. However, for those of us who believe Christianity is supposed to be done this way, and not that way, and leave the Church—or for those of us who say that we don't need to do this or that to love God, but believe we can love God in our own way—or for those of us who feel like the Church should have more bright lights, loud music, and energetic preachers and conclude the Church is too boring and ordinary for them. I say to us all, including myself—be careful brothers and sisters, for we may be falling into the same trap that the people of Nazareth did so many years ago. We may be conforming Jesus and His Church into what we believe it should be. We may be getting fooled into thinking that whatever I believe true Christianity looks like, is just fine. We may be unknowingly molding Jesus and His Church to conform to our worldly standards. We cannot allow what we think is correct, or what we think is true to pull us away from *THE truth, THE Church.*

Chapter 24: Can you handle the Truth?

There is a little saying in the coaching world that goes something like this: "Bad players want to be left alone, good players want to be coached, and the best players want to be told the truth." The bad players are the ones who don't listen to anyone, who go about their sports journey thinking they have all the answers and don't desire to hear advice or critic from anyone. The good players are those who will listen to their coach, but only really soak in what they deem as important. They like to be encouraged and praised but are selective in what coaching they take. Finally, the smallest percentage—the great ones—are the players who desire to be told the truth. Whether the truth is uplifting or a bit more painful, challenging or easy to understand, hurts their pride or builds it up. The great players are the ones who desire their coach to give them all the information they need to be great, all the things they need to do to improve. That is what the great ones desperately desire.

Sports transcend all walks of life, even the spiritual life. In a comparable image Fulton Sheen explains how different people receive truth in different ways: "If water is poured into a ditch, a glass, and a bonfire, the reaction will be quite different. So too if truth is poured into a mind that is sincere, a mind that is indifferent, and a mind that is evil, the reception will be quite different."[18] Similarly there seems, to me, to be three types of Christians—those who don't want to be coached at all, those who only take the coaching that they deem necessary, and those who desire to be told the truth. The latter, when told the truth, absorb it and after absorbing it, they use it to help them become great. Which of the three are you?

If you have questions, if you don't understand, if you just can't fathom why the Church does this or why the Church teaches that—that is ok. But don't be like the majority who are either unwilling to search for the truth, afraid of what the truth will tell them when they find it, deceived by the falsehoods of relativism, or reluctant to hear a new perspective because of stubbornness and pride. Ask questions, investigate, search, dig, and learn.

If you truly desire to find the truth, begin the journey that only the select few decide to undertake. Approach your questions and concerns with unbiased humility and you will find the truth. Whether you are outside of the Church and have yet to investigate or inside the Church and haven't taken the time to understand all that She has to offer. No matter which of the two you are, it is not so much that, right now, you believe in a lie, but (like I was) you are settling for something less than the whole truth. You are choosing not to reap all the glorious gifts that Jesus wants to give you.

If you start this journey of truth outside the Church you will soon find yourself drawn to it. If you start your journey, like me, a lukewarm, uninspired Catholic, inside the Church— you will soon find a profound love of the Catholic Church that you never before dreamed you could have. Seek the truth, and you will find it. Knock, and the doors of the Catholic Church will be opened wide to you.

4th Quarter: The Challenge

Chapter 25: What is the GOAL?

A challenge is not a challenge unless there is a goal. A game, a fight, a competition is not such, unless there is victory or defeat. There is no race unless there is a finish line. There is no journey unless there is a destination. What is a challenge without a goal? It is like 1st grade soccer where there is no score, no standings, and no champion—but everyone gets a trophy in the end. It's a delusion telling us that it doesn't matter how little effort I give, how much I don't care, or how unimportant this is to me. In other words, it's a fantasy, it's childish, and it has nothing to do with what we face in the real world—especially what we face when it comes to spiritual reality.

And here's a little reality that will knock that 1st grade participation trophy right off the shelf: 1) You are going to die. 2) You have two options after you die: Heaven or Hell. 3) What you do and don't do on this earth matters.

So before I spend the next six chapters challenging you, let's first talk about what the goal is—so that you know why you are competing in this contest in the first place. I'm sure I gave you a little indication of where I was going with this in the last paragraph with my in-your-face reality check. But, as Christians we all need to know the answer to the most important question that anyone could ever ask: What is the purpose of life? As I'm sure you have already figured out, the purpose of life is not to make a lot of money, to become famous, or own a huge house with a lot of fancy cars. It is not to get married and have kids, or to live a happy, peaceful life. And finally, the purpose of life is not (as most would try to have you believe) to "be a good person." Don't be fooled by the paths and destinations that our world tells us we need to take and achieve. There is only one ultimate goal in this life and that is to *make it to heaven!*

That's it! In the end, when it is all said and done, after the funeral and the eulogy, after the casket closes and the dirt is packed down on top of you, the only question that really matters is: Did you make it to heaven?

Our Holy Father, Pope Francis, gave us a very clear indication of this point when he said that heaven is the ultimate "goal and hope."[1] What our society teaches us is that when we see a homeless man on the street we should pity him and be glad we are not in his position. Our culture tells us when we see a rich man driving a sports car we should envy him and desire to have all he has. However, the question of who you should desire to be is not based on their living condition in this life but on their eternal living situation in the next life.

Let us remind ourselves of *The Parable of the Rich Man and Lazarus* (Luke 16:19-31). In this parable a rich man who lived for luxuries and comfort during his mortal life ended up desiring to have the eternal life of the man who laid homeless outside his door. Saint Gregory the Great commented on this parable saying, "For it was not poverty that led Lazarus to heaven, but humility; nor was it wealth that prevented the rich man from attaining eternal rest but rather his egoism and his infidelity."[2] This story isn't telling us to give up and become homeless or that if we are rich we cannot go to Heaven. But I do believe that through this parable Jesus is warning us to be careful of what we deem as most important, and to make sure that we focus not on the luxuries of this life but on the gloriousness of what an eternal life in Heaven could be like. From the mouth of a coach far greater than I, the legendary Lou Holtz once said, "For victory in life, we've got to keep focused on the goal, and the goal is heaven."[3]

With all the difficulty and struggle that we all face in our lives, how can we continue to go on? With the seemingly hopeless reality of our world today, why even attempt to make things better? With the state of our societal norms and worldly morals, why even try to live a morally upright life? With the pain and condemnation that comes with living a true Christian life, why not just give in to the culture? Why not just conform to what the world tells me to do? Why not just fall in line with what everyone else is doing? The answer is the same today as it was when Paul spoke to the Philippians, "I continue my pursuit toward the goal, the prize of God's upward calling, in Christ Jesus" (Philippians 3:14). That is the answer we can all fall back on. Why aren't we doing the things everyone else is doing? Not because we are boring or prude, not because we are self-righteous or think we are better than everyone else. It is because we are pursuing the goal that God is calling us too, because we are pursuing Heaven. A reminder from one of the greatest spiritual minds of all-time, G.K. Chesterton, "A dead thing goes with the stream. Only a living thing can go against it."[4]

"Do you not know that the runners in the stadium all run in the race, but only one wins the prize? Run so as to win. Every athlete exercises discipline in every way. They do it to win a perishable crown, but we an imperishable one" (1 Corinthians 9:24-25). We are all running the same race, we are all right now in a battle, in a fight, in the middle of our own personal marathon. We are all, at this moment, facing the greatest challenge that anyone could ever be presented with—

and we all have the opportunity to win the most cherished prize that has ever existed and that ever will exist. Don't approach this race the same way you approached your 1st grade soccer game or your 5k fun run, because this race doesn't have a participation medal. This is the most important race you will ever run, the most important fight you will ever enter. So get ready for a battle! Lock in, focus up, and "run the race as to win."

Chapter 26: Becoming a Saint

Ok, we have been given the goal, we know what we are pursuing, and we know why we are accepting the challenge. But now we must know how to reach our goal. The job of any coach is to first make their players aware of the goal that they will be pursing—and secondly, to give them the blueprint on how to achieve that goal. How do we make it to Heaven? What must we do to live eternally in the presence of Christ? Real simple, become a Saint!

"Who can ascend the mountain of the Lord? Or who may stand in his holy place? He whose hands are sinless, whose hearts are clean, who desires not what is in vain" (Psalm 24:3-4). We are told in scripture that only those whose hands are sinless, whose hearts are clean, can stand in His holy place. Jesus challenges us, "So be perfect, just as your heavenly Father is perfect" (Matthew 5:48). We have been given the blueprint by our coach, Jesus Christ. He is calling each of us to be perfect, calling each of us to holiness, calling each of us to be Saints. When I read this verse in Matthew's Gospel I sometimes imagine Jesus as Denzel Washington in *Remember the Titans*, lining us all up on the football field and bellowing in a deep and demanding coach's voice, "We will be perfect, in every aspect of the game. You drop a pass, you run a mile. You miss a blocking assignment you run a mile. You fumble the football and I will break my foot off in your John Brown hind parts—and then you will run a mile. Perfection! Let's go to work."[5] As our coach, Jesus knows what we are capable of, He knows what victory in this life means, and He presents us with what we should be pursuing—*PERFECTION!* Jesus desperately challenges us to be Saints because He desperately wants us to live eternally with Him in heaven.

In sports so often coaches present their teams with goals that are so lofty they seem almost ridiculous. During my playing career—and I'm sure most college athletes had this same experience—one of my coaches presented a challenge to our team that I knew was pretty much impossible. My freshman year of college, when I was told that we were pursuing a National Championship, I thought to myself, "that is impossible." And looking back on it now, in a sense, it pretty much was impossible or at the very least, incredibly unlikely. So why did my coach offer this goal, knowing that the likelihood of reaching the goal was nearly impossible? Why do so many coaches present ridiculously lofty goals knowing that their team will likely fail in the end? Motivational speaker Les Brown summed this question up beautifully, "Shoot for the moon, even if you miss, you'll land among the stars."[6] Coaches know that as their players pursue a daunting challenge, even if they don't achieve the goal of winning a championship, the effort given in pursuit of greatness will still be incredibly beneficial to them. C.S Lewis echoed the same message in our spiritual pursuit, "aim at heaven and you will get earth 'thrown in': aim at earth and you will get neither."[7]

The difference we have in this spiritual quest for perfection is that our coach will always make up for what we lack. Our coach guarantees us that He will get us to where we need to go as long as we strive for greatness, as long as we "run the race as to win." Let's make this very clear, for us humans, the goal of perfection, the goal of Sainthood, the goal of Heaven— is impossible. We are incapable, on our own, of becoming Saints and of going to heaven:

> "Again I say to you, it is easier for a camel to pass through the eye of a needle than for one who is rich to enter the kingdom of God." When the disciples heard this, they were greatly astonished and said, "Who then can be saved?" Jesus looked at them and said, "For human

beings this is impossible, but for God all things are possible" (Matthew 19:24-26).

The goal of Heaven and the challenge of perfection that Jesus gives to us is impossible to achieve—on our own. But, by the merits of Jesus Christ, by God's grace and our response to it, we can accomplish all that Jesus challenges us to achieve. St. Therese of Lisieux understood the human impossibility of becoming a Saint, but she also understood the promises and faithfulness of Jesus, "God could not inspire us with desires that were unrealizable, so despite my littleness I can aspire to holiness."[8]

So often, as humans, we settle for less than we are capable of. We settle for our current position at work, instead of striving for that promotion. We settle to be a good student, instead of being a great student. We decide to only pursue goals that are easily attainable, instead of pursing the ones that are most difficult. We so easily give into our human nature that tells us that the easiest path is the best path. Don't sell yourself short. You are called to greatness, in every aspect of your life—most especially, your spiritual life. All of us are called to holiness, all of us are called to be Saints, and all of us are called to spiritual greatness. Pope Benedict warns us, and then inspires us, "The world offers you comfort. But you were not made for comfort. You were made for greatness."[9]

Don't let your fear of failure or your lack of confidence hinder you from pursuing your call to greatness. Don't let your past sins or your personal vices make you think that you are not capable of becoming a Saint. "To become a Saint is not a privilege for the few but a vocation for everyone."[10] Pope Francis assures us that everyone, no matter who they are, where they come from, or what they have done, are all called to Sainthood. Each and every one of us are called to holiness. Don't let the world side track you from the goal. Don't let the devil lure you away from greatness with the worldly temptations of pleasure, power, money, and honor. Don't let the cultural norms make you stop running the race as to win. Because, as Leon Bloy once said, "The only real sadness, the only real failure, the only great tragedy in life, is not becoming a Saint."[11]

You may be thinking to yourself that you have too many flaws, too much baggage, and too much sinfulness to become a Saint. You may be thinking that it is impossible for a person like you to become holy, or that you don't have what it takes to become a Saint. You may be saying to yourself: "I'm no Mother Teresa" or "I can't be like Pope John Paul II." All those doubts that you have, are true. It is impossible for you to be holy, and you don't have what it takes to become a Saint. But all those doubts you have are doubts that leave God's help, God's guidance, and God's grace out of the equation. You, *ON YOUR OWN*, do not have what it takes to become a Saint. But as Jesus reminds us, "For human beings this is impossible, but for God all things are possible" (Matthew 19:26). God isn't asking you to be Mother Teresa. God doesn't need another St. Francis of Assisi. God needs the first Saint Kramer of Decatur, or the first Saint Emily of Boston, or the first Saint Max of Mississippi. We are all called to holiness, we are all called to be Saints. Don't be afraid of the challenge that Jesus is presenting to you, but attack it with confidence knowing that as long as you "run the race as to win," God's grace will handle the rest.

Chapter 27: Train like an Olympian

Nothing worth anything is easily grasped. No great achievement has ever come without trial and tribulation. Any accomplishment whether in sports, business, or life always comes with pain, struggle, and sacrifice. That athlete you see hosting the championship trophy was the same athlete who poured sweat in an empty gym every day for the last twenty years of their life. That valedictorian you watched give a speech at graduation was the same person who was in the library instead of the bar every Friday night for the last three years. That successful business owner is the same businessman who struggled for years trying to get their business off the ground. If you are pursuing greatness don't expect to get it without struggles, setbacks, sufferings, and pain. Those of us who achieve greatness are those of us who embrace the pains, the struggles, and the setbacks that comes with the journey.

In the midst of the struggle and pain, one of the most important aspect of becoming a Saint is simply, to truly desire to be one. Only those who wholeheartedly want to be a Saint will be able to carry on in the midst of all the setbacks and struggles that come with the pursuit of holiness. On this path towards holiness expect to encounter endless difficulties, frustrations, and trials. The ones who achieve greatness are the ones who truly want it—the ones who fall short are the ones who just say that they do. "The cause of discouragement is not the existence of difficulties, but rather the absence of a genuine desire for holiness and of reaching Heaven."[12] If you truly desire to be holy, and you wholeheartedly want to become a Saint, you will embrace all the difficulties that come with it. "Holiness is simply the application of values, principles and spirit of the Gospel to the circumstances of our everyday lives, one moment at a time. It is not complicated; it is disarmingly simple. But simple is not the same as easy."[13]

I want each of us to imagine for a moment that we are all aspiring Olympians. That we all have aspirations to make it to the next Olympics and win a gold medal. Now, as we start our journey towards our goal, we have to decide who we are going to choose to be our trainer. We choose to speak with three different trainers and they all tell us what training with them will be like, and we have to decide which trainer will best help us achieve our goal:

> **Trainer #1 says**: "I have a more modern philosophy on training. You get to decide when you want to work out and what techniques work for you. You can decide if you want to work out at the training center or if you just want to stay home. I'm not really going to challenge you to change any bad habits or push you to an uncomfortable level. This will actually be really simple, fun, and easy."

> **Trainer #2 says**: "We are going to work out three days a week, in the morning we will do a quick half hour workout and in the afternoon a longer 1 hour workout. This training will be a little tough some days, but most of the time it'll be pretty easy for you. You can still make the same life-style choices you have been making because I believe it is better to build someone up than to tear them down."

> **Trainer #3 says**: "This is going to be the hardest thing you have ever done in your entire life. We are going to work out every day for the next 3 years up until the Olympics arrive. I am going to challenge your entire way of life. You are going to change the way you eat, the way you sleep, and the things you do on your free time. You are going to think my training

methods are insane. You are going to think my rules are too strict. You are going to want to quit time and time again. But, as you know, I have years and years of experience. I have trained countless gold medalists. And I promise you, if you choose to use me as your trainer, and you commit to doing everything that I tell you to do, and you fight through the struggle and pain, you will become an Olympian!"

So, after listening to all the trainers, which of the three options are you going to choose if you really want to be an Olympian? Unless you are a gutless sissy or a spineless coward we are all going to choose trainer number three. We choose that trainer because we all know that achieving something great always requires sacrifice and struggle. To become a world-class athlete I am going to have to give up some pleasures that I used to enjoy. To become a gold medalist the path is not going to be easy, rather it will be incredibly hard. We are all spiritual athletes training to be Olympians, so that one day we will be able to stand on the Olympic podium and receive a gold medal.

So in our quest for spiritual greatness, as we pursue holiness, and embark on this seemingly impossible challenge of becoming Saints—it only makes sense that we too, must select a trainer. "Almost everyone today wants religion, but everyone wants a religion that does not cost too much; that is why Christianity has been watered down to suit the modern mind."[14] It is vital that we heed the wise words of Fulton Sheen and ask ourselves whether we are choosing the trainer who makes things easier or we are choosing the trainer that challenges us? Have we elected to go with the trainer who tells us that it's ok to take a day off or that it's ok to do things the way we want? Or have we gone with the trainer who says, "I'm more experienced than you. I know what it takes to get there. Do it my way, because I know what is best for you." If you aren't being pushed so hard by your spiritual trainer (i.e. your Church) that some days you feel like finding a new trainer who will make things easier on you, then you have chosen the wrong one. If you agree with and easily understand everything your spiritual trainer asks you to do, then you aren't being pushed out of your comfort zone—and you aren't becoming as spiritual strong as you could be.

No athlete who really wants to be great chooses a trainer who says this is going to be easy. Those get rich quick schemes are a scam. Those weight loss programs that say you are allowed to eat anything you want, news flash—they don't work! The secret and essence of the true Christian life is to give up the right to live the way you want. If you want to achieve the highest level of spirituality, if you want to become a spiritual Olympian, if you truly desire to be a Saint—wouldn't it only make sense to choose the trainer who is going to push you outside your comfort zone and who is going to challenge you to be the best you can be?

If you want to achieve spiritual greatness, make sure you have the right trainer and understand that this trainer isn't going to be easy on you. Things are going to get hard, and some days you will think you can't do it, and other days you are going to want to quit. But, "do not throw away your confidence; it will have great recompense. You need endurance to do the will of God and receive what he has promised" (Hebrews 10:35-36). Becoming holy is going to be hard, but as all the Saints in Heaven would tell you—it is worth it!

Chapter 28: Priorities

Have you ever been asked the question: "What are your top four or five priorities in your life?" I'm sure most of us have. Whether it was during a job interview, at a Church retreat, or on a governmental survey—we have all been asked the question. I remember being asked this same question in grade school. We were told to cut out pictures from magazines of the things that were most important in our life and glue them on construction paper. Then we had to explain to the class all of the things we picked and talk about where each priority stacked up on our list. I think we can all agree that priorities are very important. Whether you are an athlete, business person, parent, spouse, or student if you don't have your priorities in order things are going to go haywire.

So we are going to do a little experiment: let's all take a few minutes to think about the top four or five priorities in our life right now. Ready, Set, Go.

Now if I had to bet, I'd say almost all of us said:

1) God
2) Family
3) Friends
4) Work or School
5) Sports/Hobby/Extra Curricular Activity

No matter what walk of life or cultural background someone is from, I can almost guarantee that a large majority of people would have a very similar list. I can be even more certain that anyone who is semi-religious would have the first two or three in that order. Now when someone answers that question in this way, I think, that most people would be very impressed by the answer. I know my fourth grade teacher was very pleased with my response. It's a great way to answer the question, right? Well, I am going to argue no. And I'm sure some of you out there are probably thinking, "After reading this whole book, I'm now going to come to find that this guy is against God being first in my life? He is against me making my family the most important thing in my life besides God? Is he a lunatic or something?"

Please give me a moment to explain before you carry me off to the hills to be stoned. The problem with living by priorities is that God gets cut down and categorized as a singular priority, instead of being what He should be—your whole life. If you put God at the top of your priority list, what does that really mean? And how much priority for God is enough? Is saying my prayers in the morning and at night enough? Is going to Church on Sunday enough? Probably not.

If you were to re-write your priority list based on the time that you give to each priority, how would your list change? Because in all honesty, what you spend the most time on defines what is most important to you, doesn't it? So how would your list change if you organized it based on hours spent? It would probably look more like this:

1) Work (If you're an adult)
2) TV/Phone/Internet/Video Games
3) Family/Friends
4) Sports/Hobbies/School
5) God

I think we can all agree, that most of our priority lists would drastically change if we were to organize it based on time given to each priority.

Now, in all honesty, even the best Christian you have ever met (whose job doesn't have to do with religion) won't have God first on their list if they prioritize things by time. For example, my daily routine (most days) is to spend about the first 30 minutes of my day reading some daily passages from my Bible, reciting some of my favorite prayers, and talking to God. I usually go to adoration or daily Mass before heading into work. Then in the evening, I usually read some sort of religious book or say my prayers for about 15 minutes before I fall asleep— and I try to always say grace before eating. So let's add that time up: 30 min + 30 min + 15 min + 1 min for each meal = a total of 1 hour and 18 minutes of my day given to God. Uh-o! Where would 1 hour and 18 minutes per day stack up on my priority list? Pretty low.

But let's be real here. Anyone who has a job, goes to school, has a family, or is involved in sports realizes there is no way I can give more time to God than I give to my job or my family. If I spent seven hours a day reading the Bible and praying my kids would be neglected, I would most definitely get fired, and my wife would not be pleased with me. When Jesus asks us to give our lives to Him, when He challenges us to be holy and become Saints, is He wanting us to neglect our family? Does He want us to skip work, school, or practice? I don't think so.

Let me answer the question you are all probably asking yourself, "So what, you are telling me God doesn't want me to put Him first on my priority list? God doesn't care if my job, friends, family, school, and sport are more important to me than Him?" No! I'm not saying that at all—everyone stay calm! God is by far, without question, most definitely, without a doubt the most important thing in your life, and you should strive to treat Him that way. If you desire to become a Saint, God has to be the most important thing in your life. But even if you were able, which you are not, to give God the biggest piece of your day or week—it would still not be enough. Even if you were able to devote thirteen hours of your day to God that is still not enough to give Him what He deserves. That is still not enough to give God what He wants. God doesn't just want a piece of your day or a piece of your life. He wants all of you and every part of your life. God doesn't want to be your first priority, He wants to be the center of all your priorities.

God doesn't want to be first on the list of things you care about, He wants to be a part of and involved in everything you care about. God doesn't want you to devote five hours of your day to Him. He wants to be incorporated into every second of your day, every aspect of your life.

So when I argue and say that a person whose priority list says: 1) God 2) Family 3) Friends 4) Work/School 5) Sports; is a little bit off, I'm saying that because God doesn't want the first spot on your list of priorities. God wants to be incorporated into every spot on your list. The best analogy I have ever heard for how God should be prioritized in our lives is a baby mobile. You have seen the mobiles that parents hang above their child while they lay in the crib. These mobiles might have a bear, a plane, a basketball, a sun, a car, all connected to the mechanism in the middle that rotates them all. That is what God wants to be in your life. He wants to be the center of your mobile of life. He wants your priority list to say:

1) God in my Prayer Life
2) God within my Family
3) God a part my Friends
4) God glorified in my Work or School
5) God connected to my Sport or Hobby

God wants to be the reason that you do every other aspect of your life. He wants to be the one that makes all the other priorities in your life move. He wants everything on your life's list to revolve around Him. He wants every aspect of your life to be done through Him, with Him, by Him, and for Him.

If you want to become a spiritual Olympian, you are going to need to prioritize your life—but not in the normal way. If you want to become the Saint that Jesus is calling you to be, you must make God the center of your mobile of life. You must make God the center of your family life. You must incorporate God into all your friendships. You must attempt to glorify God through your job or your school work. You must make God a personal participant with you as you compete in a sport or pursue a hobby. If you truly desire to become holy, the only way to do so is to learn to prioritize God in a way that makes Him not just a segment of your day but allows Him to be a part of every aspect of your day and your life.

As we learned in the last chapter, we can't become Saints on our own. We can't reach our goal of Heaven without Jesus. So our only option, the only chance we have of becoming holy, is to learn to allow God to manage, guide, inspire, motivate, and lead us in every aspect of our lives.

Chapter 29: Find your Vocation

To become a Saint we all must work to align our lives to God's will. As was previously stated, we are all called to become Saints, no matter who we are. This is God's ultimate will for each of us. But we are all called to become Saints through different avenues, channels, and paths. This means we all must discern what path God is calling us to take on our walk towards eternity.

The select few, will be called to join the priesthood, become a religious sister, or join another religious order. Some of us will be called to the married life and will be asked to rear children as a part of our vocation. Still others will be called to the single life where we can use our talents and abilities to focus on the needs of those around us. God may be calling you to be a teacher or a coach, a mailman or a businesswoman. Your vocation in this life may be to be a youth minister or a lawn care professional. You may be called to live a life of turmoil or a life of luxury, a life of struggle and pain or a life of smooth sailing and comfort cruising. No matter what you are called to do in this life, no matter what your vocation in this life ends up being—your vocation has been given to you by God in order to help you achieve the goal of Heaven and to help others draw closer to God and closer to holiness.

Deep down, if we know ourselves well enough, we know what we have been called to do. It is an innate sense of self awareness that allows us to see the gifts that God has given us, and to then intern be able to discern what God is calling us to do with those gifts. But, for as much as we all think we know ourselves, no one knows us better than God. "Before I formed you in the womb I knew you, before you were born I dedicated you, a prophet to the nations I appointed you"

(Jeremiah 1:5). So in order for us to truly know ourselves we must first get to know God. And the only way you get to know God and, in turn, begin to get to know yourself, is through prayer. "It is through faithfulness to prayer that we enter into a real experience of God and a real knowledge of ourselves."[15]

What is prayer? Prayer is simply, communication with God. In the words of world renowned author Jon Gordon, "Communication is the foundation of every great relationship. Communication builds trust. Trust generates commitment. Commitment fosters teamwork, and teamwork delivers results."[16] What is prayer? Prayer is lifting our minds and hearts to God. Prayer isn't meant to conform God to our will, but conforms our will to God's. There has never been, in the history of mankind, a Saint who was not devoted and committed to their prayer life. You desire to become a Saint? Start praying—a lot!

During my junior and senior years of college I played for and was coached by my Dad. Anyone who has ever watched my Dad coach would tell you that he is a super intense, focused, driven, and disciplined guy. Most people were pretty intimidated by him after watching him coach a game. He just had a way of putting out that tough-guy coaching vibe on game day. So often people would say: "Your Dad is so intense and focused on the court, he must be really strict with you and the team." They would always want to know about the rules that he imposed on our team, expecting it to be a list as long as the scrolls of the Jewish Torah. They would always be surprised to find out that he only had three rules:

1) Show Up
2) Show Up on Time
3) Do the Best You Can

If you went back and asked every one of my teammates what our rules were on our college basketball team, they would all echo the same thing: "Show up, show up on time, do the best you can!" The reason I tell that story is because if you desire to have a profound and devout prayer life, start by doing those three things—show up, show up on time, and do the best you can. If you do you will be well on your way to becoming a prayerful Saint.

First, you must show up. If you don't show up to pray on a daily basis, you will become stagnant in your pursuit of holiness. As you stack missed prayer days together, your soul slowly begins to weaken. Only through consistent daily "showing up" will you make steady progress in your prayer life, in your relationship with Jesus, and in your understanding of God and self.

Secondly, show up on time. Not that you will be scolded or hit with a bolt of lightning if you show up late to Mass or adoration. But it is vital that you have specific times during each day that are set aside for prayer. Whether that be thirty minutes of prayer in the morning before you go to class, fifteen minutes during your lunch break to be alone with God in prayer, or an hour in the adoration chapel after work. If you don't set aside specific times each day for prayer—if you just say, "I'll pray when I have time today," you will find that you will consistently not make the time that you said you would.

Finally, do the best you can. Some days, prayer will come so easy that it will feel like the Holy Spirit is speaking for you. Some days you will feel so motivated and excited for your time of prayer that you will practically run into the chapel. However, other days you will just not feel like it. Some days your conversation with God won't come easy and your intimate time with Jesus will feel very dry. Some days your mind will wonder and your worries and stresses will try to pull your attention away from Christ. To this I tell you the same thing my Dad told our team—do the best you can, no matter the circumstances.

A consistent prayer life takes a lot of work. Devoted daily time with God is hard. But, the more consistently that you turn to our Lord in prayer, the more often you ask our Lady and the Saints to intercede on your behalf, and the more often you turn to God in praise and thanksgiving the closer you are to becoming holy. Some days you may feel too sick or too tired to pray. Some days your schedule will be so hectic that making time for prayer will be really difficult. Some days you may much rather just want to sit on the couch and watch TV instead of spending time in prayer. I'll say it again—*show up, show up on time, and do the best you can!*

Discerning God's will for you and finding out what your vocation in life is will always begin and end with a devoted prayer life. As you continually commit yourself to daily prayer, you will grow closer to God, slowly and steadily. As you grow closer to God you will find yourself growing in understanding of who you truly are. "The more we get what we now call 'ourselves' out of the way and let Him [God] take us over, the more truly ourselves we become."[17] Through a devoted prayer life you will begin to learn what your deepest desires, greatest longings, and most precious hopes and dreams really are. As you learn to lift your heart and mind to God, and as God molds your will to unite with His, soon, your vocation will come crystal clear. The more time you spend with God, the more fully you will know the mission God is calling you to. You will come to know what path God wants you to take to achieve your ultimate goal of becoming a Saint and living for all eternity in the presence of our Lord and Savior, Jesus Christ.

Chapter 30: A Full Cup Can't be Filled

After 29 (hopefully not too long or too boring) chapters, we have finally arrived back at the story that started the book, the story that inspired the title, and the story that has motivated me almost my entire life. After my Dad gave that speech at his basketball camp the summer of my 6th grade year, I found a level of motivation that I had never known before. After that day I became obsessed with becoming the best basketball player I could be. I wanted to start on the high school varsity team as a freshman. I wanted to win conference championships and a state title. From that day on, I was driven to become the best player in the state, to one day play Division 1 college basketball, and I desired more than anything to make it to the NBA. I was on a mission to achieve all the goals that I had set for myself. After hearing my Dad's speech, I understood that I didn't need to focus on the end goals, but instead focus on one thing and one thing only—filling my cup each and every day. I was a skinny, non-athletic, five-foot four-inch, twelve year old kid, but I knew what I wanted and I knew what I had to do to accomplish my goals—fill my cup, all the way to the top!

As I started on this journey to become the best basketball player I could be, I quickly realized that there were a lot of things in my life that were getting in the way of me filling my cup. As a 6th grade kid things like TV, video games, and cute girls were taking up room in my cup and weren't allowing me to put as much water in it that it was capable of holding. I began to understand that if I really wanted what I said I wanted, I would have to empty my cup before I could fill it. I had to pour out all the things in my life that were taking up space in my cup and after I did that, I would be ready to set out on my journey.

In a similar way, spiritually, we must all empty ourselves of all that hinders us from giving God our all. As always, Jesus is our perfect example. "Rather, he *emptied himself,* taking the form of a slave" (Philippians 2:7). And just as Jesus emptied himself, so too, are we called to empty ourselves of everything that binds us to this world, everything that pulls us from Jesus, anything that gets in the way of us becoming Saints. For us to receive all that God wants to give us and for us to be able to give all that we are capable of giving to God, we must rid ourselves of the things that hold us down—the things that keep us in darkness, and the things that slow us on our journey, or distract us from our goal.

Before we can *Fill Our Cup for Christ* we must first make room in our cup by getting rid of all those unimportant things that don't lead us toward Heaven. If your cup is filled with sin, it is taking up the space where grace and good works could go. If your cup is filled with selfishness, it is poking holes in your cup and slowing draining out the water you're trying to put in it. If your cup is filled with anger, jealousy, depression, fear, or loneliness there is less room for joy, thanksgiving, praise, and courage. "We increase our capacity for grace as we empty the sand out of the bottle, as we remove the obstacles to grace which clutter up our soul."[18] Everyone is different, some of us may have cups filled with pornography and drunkenness. For some the rocks in our cup may be obsession of money, clothes, or cars. Still others may have cups filled with the sharp edges of gossip, slander, or bullying. No matter who we are or what vices fill our cups, we must all ask for the grace to pour out the things that are taking up space in our lives, all the things that are poking holes in our cup.

Emptying your cup means going against the grain. Riding your life of sin means being abnormal. Living a life of virtue means not conforming to what our culture tells us is good, ok, or cool. If you desire to be a Saint you have to empty your cup—and in the motivational words of author, Dan Dematte, by doing that you are actually now becoming a rebel:

> "It is no longer rebellious to drink and have sex. It is no longer rebellious to cuss and disrespect authority. It is no longer rebellious to sin and live in darkness. Sin is not rebellion; it is conformity. If you're steeped in materialism, selfishness, and sin, you are just a conformist. If you want to be a rebel, if you want to be revolutionary, you need to be a Saint. The Saints are the real rebels—they are the ones doing what no one else is doing. In this corrupt generation, it's rebellious to go to daily Mass, to read your Bible, to live virtuously, to defend the truth, and to live in the light. That's rebellion!"[19]

Each of us needs to take a long hard look at the sins that fill our lives. Through prayer, petition, constant trips to confession, fasting, and almsgiving we will find the strength, by the grace of God, to throw out all the things in our life that separate us from Christ. We will find the holy motivation to mend the holes in our cups that have been punctured by sin. We will find the courage to lift up our cups and pour out everything in our life that prevents us from putting as much water in it as it can possibly hold. Don't be afraid to go against the grain, to swim against the current, to be a rebel. Don't be afraid to empty your cup. Don't be afraid to be a Saint.

Chapter 31: Fill Your Cup for Christ

Whether we realize it or not, each of us have been given incredibly important gifts. Each of us have been given certain talents meant to be used for God's glory and for the sake of His kingdom. Some of us have been given very obvious talents—such as communication talents, artistic talents, athletic talents, or intellectual talents. If you are one of these, congratulations, you have been given a very big cup by God. However, some of us might find it much more difficult to locate our talent. Some of us may have the talent of patience or the gift of listening. Some may be talented in prayer, or have a generous heart, or a strong love of the poor. Others may have a great smile, great laugh, or a beautiful outlook on life. For those of us who struggle to find our God-given talent—you may have been given a little bit smaller cup then the others. Just like me, the five-foot four-inch, non-athletic aspiring basketball player was given a very small cup, you too may have been given a smaller sized cup when compared to the rest. But just as my Dad told me I will tell you, that is irrelevant! That does not matter! Whether you have a 64 oz. gas station guzzler for a cup, or whether your talent can be summed up by a Dixie cup, that is not what is important. All that matters is that you fill your cup to the top for Christ.

We all, as Christians, play a role in the one body of Christ's Church, and we all play different roles to spread the Gospel to all the earth. As Paul explained to the Corinthians, "For in one Spirit we were all baptized into one body, whether Jews or Greeks, slaves or free persons, and we were all given to drink of one Spirit" (1 Corinthians 12:13). No matter if the talent we each have been given can be described as a big cup or a small cup, we are all a part of the same body. Even if you feel like what you have to offer is insignificant compared to others, you are a member of Christ's body and play a vital role in helping to fulfill God's will "on earth as it is in Heaven." "If a foot should say, 'Because I am not a hand I do not belong to the body,' it does not for this reason belong any less to the body. Or if an ear should say, 'Because I am not an eye I do not belong to the body,' it does not for this reason belong any less to the body. If the whole body were an eye, where would the hearing be? If the whole body were hearing, where would the sense of smell be? But as it is, God placed the parts, each one of them, in the body as He intended" (1 Corinthians 15-18). As a baptized Christian, it is irrelevant whether you are a hand or a foot, whether you are a big lung or a tiny eyelash. Each member of the body, no matter if he or she be big or small, plays a vital role in the stability and growth of the body. "Indeed, the parts of the body that seem to be weaker are all the more necessary, and those parts of the body that we consider less honorable we surround with greater honor, and our less presentable parts are treated with greater priority" (1 Corinthians 12:22-23).

Although your cup may be smaller than your neighbors and you may feel like your vocation, your occupation, your calling in this life is insignificant when it comes to the growth and advancement of God's kingdom—it is not. "The great challenge is not to succeed in the world's eyes, but rather discover what your unique abilities are and offer them to the world in the best way you can."[19] Whether you are a famous Christian singer, a youth minister, a basketball coach, or a school janitor you are a member of Christ's body and you play a vital role in the master plan that God is unfolding to save the souls of all the world. We have all been given certain talents, and certain opportunities to help bring others closer to Christ. We have all been put in a certain place, a particular occupation, and have been called to a certain vocation in order to spread God's

Kingdom to all the earth. It makes no difference if you have the influence and platform of a famous athlete or that of a coal miner. It makes no difference if what you do and say is seen and heard by millions or by no one. Whether you are giving a speech to the masses or saying a quiet pray to end abortion, you are making a difference in God's Kingdom.

The late/great Kobe Bryant and fellow Catholic stated in a 2015 interview, "I've always said that I wanted to be remembered as a player that didn't waste a moment, didn't waste a day..."[21] In relation to eternity every moment matters, every day can be used for the glory of God. One friendly smile to a stranger makes a difference in the Kingdom. One kind word to the saddened and despaired makes a difference. A simple acknowledgment of the homeless man on the corner makes a difference. The parent who comes home after work exhausted, but still musters up the energy to play with their kids, contributes to God's master plan. One small petition, one prayed rosary, one lit candle, one offered Mass, can and does, have profound effects on eternity.

As the great Martin Luther King Jr. once said, "If it falls your lot to be a street sweeper, sweep streets like Michelangelo painted pictures, like Shakespeare wrote poetry, like Beethoven composed music; sweep streets so well that all the host of Heaven and earth will have to pause and say, 'Here lived a great street sweeper, who swept his job well."[22] No matter your talent. No matter your occupation or influence. No matter the size of your cup. As long as you fill that cup each day and do whatever you are called to do for the glory of God and the glory of His Kingdom—you are doing God's will and you are well on your way to becoming a Saint.

> "It will be as when a man who was going on a journey called in his servants and entrusted his possessions to them.

To one he gave five talents; to another, two; to a third, one—to each according to his ability. Then he went away.

Immediately the one who received five talents went and traded with them, and made another five.

Likewise, the one who received two made another two.

But the man who received one went off and dug a hole in the ground and buried his master's money.

After a long time the master of those servants came back and settled accounts with them.

The one who had received five talents came forward bringing the additional five. He said, 'Master, you gave me five talents. See, I have made five more.'

His master said to him, 'Well done, my good and faithful servant. Since you were faithful in small matters, I will give you great responsibilities. Come, share your master's joy.'

[Then] the one who had received two talents also came forward and said, 'Master, you gave me two talents. See, I have made two more.'

His master said to him, 'Well done, my good and faithful servant. Since you were faithful in small matters, I will give you great responsibilities. Come, share your master's joy.'

Then the one who had received the one talent came forward and said, 'Master, I knew you were a demanding person, harvesting where you did not plant and gathering where you did not scatter; so out of fear I went off and buried your talent in the ground. Here it is back.'

His master said to him in reply, 'You wicked, lazy servant! So you knew that I harvest where I did not plant and gather where I did not scatter?

Should you not then have put my money in the bank so that I could have got it back with interest on my return?

Now then! Take the talent from him and give it to the one with ten.

For to everyone who has, more will be given and he will grow rich; but from the one who has not, even what he has will be taken away. And throw this useless servant into the darkness outside, where there will be wailing and grinding of teeth'" (Matthew 25:14-30).

As we contemplate this parable given to us by Jesus, we must reflect on which of the three servants we are. In the parable we see that it is irrelevant to the master how many talents each had been given. Instead, what was important to the master was what they did with the talents that they had been given. In the same way, each of us have been given a certain number of talents—a certain sized cup. All that our 'Master' requires of us is that we do our very best to get the most out of what we have been given. Let's imagine for a moment that the servant who received five talents only made two more instead of five. And let's say that the servant with one talent made one more. I believe, that although the servant who was given five talents made more than the servant who was given one, the master would have been far more pleased with the servant who only made one talent—for that servant made the most out of what he was given. He filled his cup to the top.

Success and failure in life is very simple. Success and failure in the spiritual realm is also extremely simple. Each one of us have been given a certain sized cup. Some of us may have cups the size of a carton of milk and others the size of a thimble. However, all that matters in this life is whether or not you fill your cup to the top. If you have a huge cup but only fill it half way to the top, you are not fulfilling God's plan for you. If you decide to only give partial effort as a spouse or a parent, as an employee or a student. If you decide to do the bare minimum when it comes to your faith life, you have failed and you have become like the wicked servant in the parable—burying your talent in the ground. If you have a small cup but fill your cup to the top, you are fulfilling God's plan for you. If you decide that although you don't have a whole lot to offer, you are still going to do all you can to be the best mom, dad, son, daughter, or friend you can be. If you realize that although your talents are limited or your influence small, you can still do the little things that make a big difference—you have succeeded and have become like the first two servants in the parable.

As you walk on your path towards heaven and embark on your journey to become a Saint don't be fearful of failure. Because there is no such thing as failure for those who fill their cup to the top for Christ. "Membership among the followers of Jesus Christ does not require perfection. But it does require us to strive to live as Jesus invites us to live. And that mean's working diligently to close the gap."[23] No matter if we achieve greatness or live a life of struggles and defeats, the definition of true success lies not in the outcome of the fight but in what you have put into the fight along the way. Saint Mother Teresa summed up what God expects of us when she said, "God doesn't require us to succeed, He only requires that you try."[24] At the end of this life, when you come face to face with our Lord and Savior on judgement day—if you can stand before the person that you love most and say, "See Lord, I filled my cup to the top for you," you will surely hear back in the most loving and joyful voice, "Well done, my good and faithful servant! Come, share your master's joy!"

Eighteen years ago, without even realizing it, my life changed for the better. A simple story and a short ride home with my Father planted a seed in my heart that directed me throughout my entire basketball career and continues to inspire me to this day. That unknown spiritual seed that was planted in the summer of 2002 laid dormant in my soul for almost half my life. But finally, through the cultivation and fertilization of experiences in life and sport, through tribulation and triumph, victories and defeat, friends and family, and most especially by the glorious grace of God—a flower began to bloom. The journey that began with a 6th grade kid desperately trying to become the best basketball player he could be turned into a no-named Division 3 assistant basketball coach attempting to become a Saint. Not a day goes by that I don't think about filling my cup. While on this journey I have come to understand that to be a success in this life, to become the Saint I am called to be, all I have to do is fill my cup to the top each and every day. Eighteen years later, I'm still trying my best to fill my cup—as a basketball coach, as a husband, as a father, and most importantly as a Christian.

Thank you for coming on this spiritual journey with me. I hope and pray that by God's grace you will grow in love and relationship with Jesus; that you will find the strength to endure through your trials; that you will seek the truth; and that one day you will become the Saint that God is calling you to be. And remember brothers and sisters—all that matters in this life is that each day when you open your eyes and lift your head off that pillow, you focus all your energy and all your effort on one thing...

Filling Your Cup, *to the top*, for Christ!

Jesus,

Today, make me constantly aware of Your presence, & continually attentive to Your perfect & holy will.

As I offer this day & my entire self to You, allow me to glorify Your name in my thoughts, words, actions, & prayers.

Teach me to surrender like You & Your mother surrendered. Through my surrender, teach me to accept all that comes my way...

The good & the bad, the joyful & sorrowful, the mundane & the extra ordinary.

Allow me to do all these things out of great thanksgiving, joy, & unceasing love for You.

I love you Jesus, take care of everything.

Acknowledgments

As a first time author that had no idea what in the world I was getting myself into when I began the process of writing this book, I would be remised if I didn't take the time to thank all the wonderful people who made this book come to life.

Thank you to all the self-giving priests who helped critic, edit, and revise this book. Special thanks to Father Michael Giesler (priest of the Prelature Opus Dei) for his guidance throughout this process. The time, detail, and care he put into the early revisions of this book is a testament to the man he is and the mission of Opus Dei. To Father Joe Molloy (Pastor of Holy Family Catholic Church) who helped with the early editing process and has been a wonderful steward of God for me and my family.

Thank you to Lauren Barnhorst who willingly offered her talents as a digital media artist and created the amazingly beautiful cover for this book.

To all my family and friends who supported me throughout this process with words of encouragement, advice, and most especially constant and continual lifting up in prayer.

Finally, to my amazing wife, Andrea, the rock of our family, the wonderful mother of our three perfect children, and the love of my life. Through all the ups and downs this life has thrown at us you have been my constant, steady, and loving companion. I love you, forever and ever.

Notes

Footnote: Many of the shorter or more well-known quotes in this book were originally discovered through social media posts and/or online search engines, which are available to anyone interested in doing further research and investigation.

1st Quarter: The Motivation

1. *Pope John Paul II (1979). "Pilgrim of Peace: The Homilies and Addresses of His Holiness Pope John Paul II on the Occasion of His Visit to the United States of America*
2. *https://gabriel-theotokos.blogspot.com/2012/03/24-march-2012-our-lady-of-dove.html
3. Francis Fernandez, *In Conversation with God: Volume 2* (New Rochelle, Scepter, 2015), p. 176
4. Unknown Quote Location
5. Unknown Source
6. Scott Hahn, *The Lamb's Supper* (New York, Image, 1999), p. 127-128
7. *https://saintlyquotations.blogspot.com/2013/07/wisdom-from-st-teresa-of-avila.html
8. *OLGCPlymouth. "RCIA Week 2 - God the Father." *YouTube*, 30 Sept.2013,(1:41:50-1:41:58), https://www.youtube.com/watch?v=ArZGDlCqFlQ&t=3738s
9. Joseph F. Girzone, *A Portrait of Jesus* (New York, Doubleday, 1998), p. 75

10. Unknown Quote Location – *Permission Granted by Fr. John Ricardo*
11. Max Lucado, *Just Like Jesus* (Nashville, Thomas Nelson, 2003), p. 3-4
12. *Compendium: Catechism of the Catholic Church* (Washington D.C, USCCB, 2008), p. 161
13. Max Lucado, *Just Like Jesus* (Nashville, Thomas Nelson, 2003), p. 53
14. Brother Lawrence & Frank Lauback, *Practicing His Presence* (Jacksonville, SeedSowers), p. 10
15. Max Lucado, *Just Like Jesus* (Nashville, Thomas Nelson, 2003), p. 58
16. *Compendium: Catechism of the Catholic Church* (Washington D.C, USCCB, 2008), p. 168
17. Brother Lawrence & Frank Lauback, *Practicing His Presence* (Jacksonville, SeedSowers), p. 15
18. Joseph F. Girzone, *A Portrait of Jesus* (New York, Doubleday, 1998), p. 81
19. Brother Lawrence & Frank Lauback, *Practicing His Presence* (Jacksonville, SeedSowers), p. 19
20. *https://libquotes.com/mother-teresa/quote/lbe1z1j
21. Saint Josemaria Escriva, The Way – Furrow – The Forge, (New York, Scepter, 2011), p. 205
22. Brother Lawrence & Frank Lauback, *Practicing His Presence* (Jacksonville, SeedSowers), p. 15-16
23. *Compendium: Catechism of the Catholic Church* (Washington D.C, USCCB, 2008), p. 166
24. Brother Lawrence & Frank Lauback, *Practicing His Presence* (Jacksonville, SeedSowers), p. 27
25. Brother Lawrence & Frank Lauback, *Practicing His Presence* (Jacksonville, SeedSowers), p. 59
26. *Francis, Pope (Pontifex). 4 April 2013. Tweet.
27. From Saint Louis' Advice to His Son, in Medieval Civilization, trans. and eds. Dana Munro and George Clarke Sellery (New York: The Century Company, 1910), pp. 366 -75.

2nd Quarter: The Trial

1. *https://www.goodreads.com/quotes/214071-i-think-there-is-no-suffering-greater-than-what-is
2. *http://fathervenditti.com/3-7-2019.htm
3. *https://www.goodreads.com/author/quotes/355231.John_Vianney
4. Matthew Kelly, *Rediscover Jesus* (Erlanger, Beacon, 2015), p. 74
5. *Keller, Tiimothy (timkellernyc). 21 Dec 2014, 2:42 PM. Tweet. https://twitter.com/timkellernyc/status/546767582779674624
6. Fulton J. Sheen, *Way to Inner Peace* (Garden City, Garden City, 1955), p. 22
7. *https://stephensmiracle.blogspot.com/
8. Anthony De Mello, *Awareness* (New York, Image, 1990), p. 6
9. Sarah Young, *Jesus Calling* (Nashville, HarperCollins, 2004), p. 229
10. Sarah Young, *Jesus Calling* (Nashville, HarperCollins, 2004), p. 230
11. Joseph F. Girsone, *Never Alone* (New York, Doubleday, 1995), p. 14
12. Dale Ahlquist, *All Roads* (The American Chesterton Society, 2014), p. 79
13. Pope John Paul II (1999). "Celebrate the Third Millennium!: Facing the Future with Hope", Servant Publications
14. Sarah Young, *Jesus Calling* (Nashville, HarperCollins, 2004), p. 241
15. Sarah Young, *Jesus Lives* (Nashville, Thomas Nelson, 2009), p. 8
16. Sarah Young, *Jesus Calling* (Nashville, HarperCollins, 2004), p. 257
17. C.S. Lewis, *Mere Christianity* (New York, HarperCollins, 2001), p. 56
18. Matthew Kelly, *Rediscover Catholicism* (Erlanger, Beacon, 2010), p. 231

19. Sarah Young, *Jesus Calling* (Nashville, HarperCollins, 2004), p. 264 & 265

3rd Quarter: The Truth

1. Scott & Kimberly Hahn, *Rome Sweet Home* (San Francisco, Ignatius Press, 1993), p. 9
2. Scott & Kimberly Hahn, *Rome Sweet Home* (San Francisco, Ignatius Press, 1993), p. 42
3. Matthew Kelly, *Rediscover Catholicism* (Erlanger, Beacon, 2010), p. 201
4. Francis Fernandez, *In Conversation with God: Volume 2* (New Rochelle, Scepter, 2015), p. 426
5. OLGCPlymouth. "RCIA Week 17: The Eucharist." *YouTube*, 25 Feb.2014,(56:45-57:12), https://www.youtube.com/watch?v=hok6cQ3sDxs
6. *https://www.catholicnewsagency.com/news/pope-without-the-eucharist-everything-the-church-does-is-vain-71974
7. Francis Fernandez, *In Conversation with God: Volume 2* (New Rochelle, Scepter, 2015), p. 342
8. Barron, Bishop Robert. "Bishop Barron's Sermons." Audio blog post. What Does It Mean to Say that Christ is King? Word on Fire, 20 Nov. 2018. Web. 20 Jan. 2019.
9. Unknown Location of Quote – *Permission by Fr. John Ricardo*
10. Fulton J. Sheen, *Way to Inner Peace* (Garden City, Garden City, 1955), p. 71
11. Anthony De Mello, *Awareness* (New York, Image, 1990), p. 18
12. Matthew Kelly, *Rediscover Catholicism* (Erlanger, Beacon, 2010), p. 9-10
13. Scott & Kimberly Hahn, *Rome Sweet Home* (San Francisco, Ignatius Press, 1993), preface. Xi
14. Christopher West, *Good News about Sex and Marriage* (Cincinnati: Servant, 2007), p. 23.
15. *https://www.goodreads.com/quotes/575431-once-you-were-a-child-once-you-knew-what-inquiry

16. Matthew Kelly, *Rediscover Catholicism* (Erlanger, Beacon, 2010), p. 283
17. Fulton J. Sheen, *Way to Inner Peace* (Garden City, Garden City, 1955), p. 71
18. Fulton J. Sheen, *Way to Inner Peace* (Garden City, Garden City, 1955), p. 148

4th Quarter: The Challenge

1. *Pope Francis, General Audience, 25 October 2017. https://www.ncregister.com/daily-news/pope-francis-heaven-is-the-ultimate-goal-of-our-hope
2. *https://catholicfaithpatronsaints.com/prayers-quips-and-quotes-st-gregory-the-great-feast-day-sept-4/
3. *https://www.azquotes.com/quote/698472
4. Dale Ahlquist, *All Roads* (The American Chesterton Society, 2014), p. 43
5. *Remember the Titans*. Dir. Boaz Yakin. Perf. Denzel Washington. Disney, 2000.
6. *https://www.brainyquote.com/quotes/les_brown_383867
7. C.S. Lewis, *Mere Christianity* (New York, HarperCollins, 2001), p. 134
8. Jacques Philippe, *The Way of Trust and Love* (New York, Scepter, 2012), p. 9
9. *https://thosecatholicmen.com/articles/made-for-greatness/
10. *Francis, Pope (Pontifex). 21 Nov 2013, 8:21 AM. Tweet. https://twitter.com/Pontifex/status/403528682800562176
11. *https://www.goodreads.com/quotes/8319180-the-only-real-sadness-the-only-real-failure-the-only
12. Francis Fernandez, *In Conversation with God: Volume 2* (New Rochelle, Scepter, 2015), p. 479
13. Matthew Kelly, *Rediscover Catholicism* (Erlanger, Beacon, 2010), p. 54
14. Fulton J. Sheen, *Way to Inner Peace* (Garden City, Garden City, 1955), p. 92

15. Jacques Philippe, *The Way of Trust and Love* (New York, Scepter, 2012), p. 84
16. Jon Gordon & Mike Smith, *You Win in the Locker Room First* (Hoboken, John Wiley & Sons, 2015), p. 51
17. C.S. Lewis, *Mere Christianity* (New York, HarperCollins, 2001), p. 225
18. Leo Trese, *The Faith Explained* (New York, Scepter, 1965), p. 429
19. Dan Dematte, *Holiness Revolution* (Hebron, Beacon, 2012), p. 28
20. Matthew Kelly, *Perfectly Yourself* (North Palm Beach, Beacon, 2017), p. 33
21. *ESPN (@espn). 27 Jan 2020, 8:39 AM. Tweet. https://twitter.com/espn/status/1221804834380296193
22. *https://www.goodreads.com/quotes/21045-if-a-man-is-called-to-be-a-street-sweeper
23. Matthew Kelly, *Rediscover Jesus* (Erlanger, Beacon, 2015), p. 113
24. *https://www.goodreads.com/quotes/16809-god-doesn-t-require-us-to-succeed-he-only-requires-that